BODY
TALK

Clarkson
Potter/
Publishers
New York

BODY TALK

How to Embrace Your Body and Start Living Your Best Life

KATIE STURINO

Illustrations by Monica Garwood

THIS BOOK IS FOR <u>LITTLE KATIE</u>—MY MASCOT, NOT MY VAGINA.

It's also for women and girls everywhere. May we free ourselves from the hamster wheel of body hate so that we can live out our wildest and weirdest dreams.

Little Katie

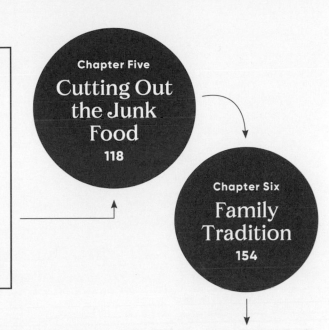
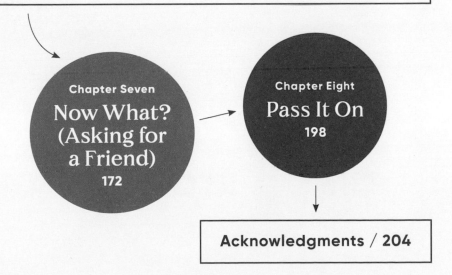

THE · STORY · OF

G

MY

LIFE

(as opposed
to the 1988
movie starring
Tom Hanks)

I didn't always think being big was a bad thing. Until I went to kindergarten, I was encouraged to "eat up" and grow big and strong. I was barely aware of my body beyond its most basic elements (head, shoulders, knees, and toes, knees and toes). So long as I could run around barefoot in my fish-printed swimsuit and cartwheel for hours on the front lawn, I was happy. My body was just along for whatever ride I wanted to go on.

*My body was just along for whatever
ride I wanted to go on*

"At age nine, I had to wear my soccer coach's jersey during games."

I started to become aware of my body, its bigness, and the so-called problem with its bigness only when others began pointing it out to me. At five years old, I was voted "Heaviest Kid" in class after my peers and I were weighed (literally weighed, like on a scale in front of everyone) in part of some sort of deranged school-superlative activity. That same year, my gymnastics coach told my mom I was too big for the sport. When I was seven, my doctor put me on a diet.

At age nine, I had to wear my soccer coach's jersey during games because the uniform company didn't make my size—which, in terms of humiliation level, is the wearable athletic equipment equivalent of accidentally calling a teacher "Mommy" in front of the whole class. My elderly female neighbor commented on my "developing figure" when I was ten. A year later, the boys in my class began commenting on it, too.

It was disorienting to learn that I didn't just *have* a body—

in the eyes of others, I WAS my body.

It defined me. It was even more disorienting to learn that my body (and therefore I) wasn't considered the "right" size or shape. Shame began eating away at my confidence as I began to realize my body wasn't considered normal, and in one way or another, it was being judged.

I've always felt like the biggest person in the room. I felt ashamed of that fact until I was thirty-three. Growing up (in Wisconsin— go Badgers!), I had plenty of wonderful, supportive people in my life. I am lucky to have parents who raised me with the kindness, enthusiasm, love, and care one might typically bestow upon a baby rescue animal before releasing it into the wild. But a lot of people in my life—phenomenal humans that they were and are— unintentionally reinforced the very insecurities I was developing. For all the love and wisdom I received, no one ever said to me, "Your size does not determine your worth" or "When you grow up, you do not have to look like the women you see on TV to be successful." No one said, "You're just a kid" or even "What matters is who you are, not what size you are."

It's no one's fault they didn't say these things to me. I blame long-standing Societal Beauty Standards, but that's another story for another page (page 137, to be exact). And while I can't help but think about how different my relationship with my own body growing up would have been if someone had just said, "There is nothing wrong with you," in 2015, I learned to say it to myself. And then everything changed.

Toast

My life used to revolve around three different worlds: my clients, my ex-husband, and my dogs. I ran my own public relations company,* where my daily goal was to uplift and champion my clients. In my off-hours, however, I rarely uplifted or championed myself. Because my self-esteem was so low, and I was used to it being so low, I found it a lot safer to raise everyone else's star instead of mine. Though I ran my own business, promoting my then-husband's burgeoning career took priority and the majority of my focus. And my beloved dog, Toast, who is no longer with us but will forever bark at the doorbell of my heart—well, she was a canine celebrity, which made me her manager, or her dogager, as I called myself (. . . as a joke, but also I was dead serious).

A big part of Toast's career was dedicated to animal rescue. Through her Instagram account,** media presence, and event appearances, Toast helped to raise awareness about the horrors of puppy mills and encouraged animal lovers to "adopt, don't shop." Whenever people would say to me "What you do for animals is so

---

* Tinder PR. I named it years before app-based online dating took off, but once it did, you can imagine the kinds of misdirected emails I received.

** When Toast passed away in 2017, I was devastated, but I also felt so lucky to have had her in my life. I know that a lot of people say their dogs are their best friends, but Toast was like my angel on earth. I wanted to find a way to honor her legacy and continue our animal activism (while also showcasing the rest of my cute dogs, Toast's less-famous sisters), so I changed the name of the Instagram account from @ToastMeetsWorld to @DogMeetsWorld, where I frequently pay tribute to Toast's sweet memory.

amazing," I'd correct them: "Well, it's all Toast." It was all Toast! After all, people didn't show up to charity events to see me. I wasn't the cute rescue Cavalier King Charles Spaniel with a silky chestnut coat, no teeth, the disposition of a calm angel, and a lovely, permanently lolling tongue! And why would anyone ever want to hear from me, anyway? Even to myself, I was no one.

My self-perception began to shift shortly after I accompanied Toast to a video shoot for a fashion blog called Man Repeller. As usual, Toast was there to be an adorable, front-and-center star. I was there to manage (dogage) her affairs behind the scenes. While watching Toast do her thing, I got to talking with a woman named Amelia Diamond, a writer for Man Repeller at the time (who has since become a lifelong friend—aw!). We bonded right away because of our shared sense of humor and mutual recognition that we have identical foreheads. There was such an immediate comfort between us that I allowed myself to push out a small, secret wish (did you think I was about to say "fart"?): I told her that I wanted to be photographed for the site. Me! A woman who had never fit into her chosen industry, literally and metaphorically—who never felt she could "pull off" certain styles she always secretly wanted to try.

When you're used to pushing for the success of others but never for yourself, you almost can't believe it when you *do* take a flier, promote yourself, and receive back a giant "Yes!" like the one Amelia gave me. After it registered that she had in fact said yes,

My insecurities could NO LONGER hurt me.

my internal reaction was "What have I done?" I had to actually be photographed? In clothes? With my rolls and chub and jiggle and flub threatening to ruin the shoot?

I was so uncomfortable in front of the camera on the day of—"Do I have a double chin? Do I look like I don't belong? Do I look enormous? What about now? Now do I have a double chin???"— that the team had to distract me with tactics usually reserved for crying toddlers on Santa's lap. I felt like a clumsy bear in a tutu. But when the article was published, the comments told a different story. Readers were thrilled to see a body that looked like mine. A body that looked like theirs! In cool clothes!! On a fashion blog that I had long read for my own style inspiration!!! It was my big aha moment, my "Eureka!" A switch flipped and the light turned on: My body was not, and is not, the problem.

My BODY was NOT,

and is NOT, the PROBLEM?! Holy. Shit.

That realization, paired with the commenters' enthusiasm, gave me the courage I needed to launch an Instagram account that would pass the message on to other women. I called it The 12ish Style because I wore a size 12-ish at the time, but I had no idea that as my weight began to rise, I'd learn to accept my body as I never had before and would eventually speak about body acceptance

of all kinds to an audience of women who came in all shapes and sizes. Shortly after the Instagram account began taking off, I created a blog to give myself more room to dive deeper into the topics I cared about. Writing about how hard it was to find cool jeans that fit me led me to larger conversations about the lack of size representation in fashion, retail, the media, and pop culture. The deeper I dove, the louder my new internal mantra became: MY BODY IS NOT THE PROBLEM.

I started taking pride in what I previously found embarrassing about my body: I went from hiding the fact that I waxed my upper lip to waxing it live on Instagram. I went from covering my melasma with skin-matching concealer to preventing it with a blue zinc mustache so ferocious it could rival the 'stache of Tom Selleck. I went from not wearing shorts in public to wearing thongs on the beach. I talk about poop all the time. (I share, probably more than anyone wants me to, about the post-coffee panic of having to poop midwalk with no bathrooms in sight.) The old me never would have dared admit I had hair follicles or sweat glands. The new me started a product line to solve things like thigh chafe, boob sweat, foot odor, and butt acne. Then I wrapped it up in super cute packaging and called it MegaBabe. More on that in a few seconds—and later on in the book (see page 189).

I didn't intend to become an activist for body acceptance, but that's exactly what happened, thanks to the incredible community of women who encouraged me to keep going, keep talking, and keep exposing the things that make us feel ashamed for what they really are: bullshit illusions. Throughout the process, I learned just how therapeutic it was to talk about this stuff with people who could relate. "You have boob sweat? I have boob sweat! I thought that was just me." To borrow a line from scammy diet advertisements, the shame "just melted right off!"

The more comfortable I got talking about my body shame, the more I started to overcome it. I began to understand that everything I'd ever felt body-shameful about was nothing to actually be ashamed of. The perfect body, I was starting to learn, wasn't real. It was a societally created illusion. With every post I put up that highlighted my formerly self-perceived flaws, I began to feel my own power rising up from within. It was like heartburn, if heartburn felt good.

My insecurities could no longer hurt me. It gave me the confidence to start the beauty line I just started telling you about, MegaBabe, which makes solutions for the kinds of bodily problems I used to find embarrassing, like thigh chafe. I figured if they were problems I had, others might have them, too. (And, as it turns out, no matter your weight, shape, or size, if you're a person with skin that rubs against skin, you *know* about chafing.) Shedding my shame, building up my self-esteem, learning that I was worthy of love and success and cool clothes—these realizations changed my life. They helped me rediscover the joy of the little girl inside me who loved nothing more than running around on a very public-facing lawn in her favorite bathing suit. Probably with a wedgie.

We all have our individual stories about the first time we realized our own bodies weren't "acceptable." What about you? Were you bullied by a group of insecure tweens? Did a family member make a hurtful comment? Did a kid in your class give you a funny nickname? Were you the only one who didn't find that nickname funny? Did that nickname stick?

Maybe it happened in a store—were you told that you didn't have the right body for that brand's clothes? I've learned over the years that I wasn't alone in any of these experiences. Most of us lacked positive body reinforcement when we were young. But you know what? We all have the power to rebuild that confidence in ourselves.

In order to heal, we must recognize the moments that have built up like grime on bathroom tiles. It's going to suck a little, but I'm going to help you do that. And then—*then* I'm gonna help you power-wash that crap away. I am writing this book to help heal the little girl inside you who was told her appearance was wrong—to revive the joy she used to feel before she gave up on all the fun things she loved because it felt safer to hide. You're still her, you know. She's still in there. We just have to remind her how good it feels to do cartwheels with one of her butt cheeks hanging out.

THE CLASSROOM OGRE

My nickname in middle school was Ogre. A boy in my class said it *one time*, and just like that, the name caught on.

I already felt like a monster—the name confirmed it. (Keep in mind this was eleven years before a popular animated fairy tale made ogres cute.) It made me feel awful, and I hated everything about it, but I rolled with it because I wanted to be liked. I wanted to seem chill.

A few years later, I pulled some of my friends aside and asked them to stop calling me Ogre. They did, and, over time, everyone seemed to forget about it . . .

Except for me, because here we are! The name stuck. So did some of the associated emotions. I still feel like an embarrassed middle-schooler when I tell this story, but the embarrassment dissipates when I remind myself that (A) I am not an ogre. (B) I am cool as shit. And (C) Even if I were an ogre, guess what? They're cool as shit, too! And they have excellent singing voices.

How to Use This Book: A Somewhat Obvious Manual

If you're holding this book, it's for you. We all have insecurities about our physical appearance. Every single one of us. If it's not our size or our weight or our cellulite or our shape, it's our nose, lips, teeth, ears, belly (and buttons), new-to-you postpartum bodies, head hair, arm hair, toe hair, leg hair, pubic hair— anything that grows out of our pores, really, which leads us into pimples, whiteheads, blackheads, chin whiskers, nipple whiskers . . . and speaking of nipples, our nipples, our boobs, butts, knees, thighs, shins, calves, eyes (and brows and lashes and lids and dark circles and eye bags, etc.), nails, scars, rash-prone skin, rosacea, dermatitis, skin tags, stretch marks, sweaty pits, hyperhidrosis, hips, vulvas! . . . the list goes on and on. In fact, opposite is a space to add some specifics of your own just so you KNOW this book is for you if you could use a pep talk or two.

Trust me: I could have written this whole book about what it was like to be a fourteen-year-old with a full mustache. This book is for everyone who's tired of thinking about their so-called body issues, whatever those may be. It's for anyone who'd much rather move on with her damn day and have a good life!

WHAT DO YOU HATE ABOUT YOUR BODY? GO AHEAD, LET IT OUT!

Having insecurities is nothing to be ashamed of (for the love of all things good, let's not add yet another thing to the shame list). No matter your relationship with your physical being, you are powerful, unstoppable, fun, and worthy of love. This book is here to help reinforce the message that all those things are already inside you. It's yours to return to whenever you need a reminder of what you already know you know: that your appearance doesn't determine your worth.

Is this book a magical cure-all? No.

Think of this book as a tool to help you push through the endless bullshit and free up valuable headspace so that you can focus on the things you'd rather be doing—the things that bring you joy. Imagine a world that has evolved past the "body conversation," or at least a world in which you've evolved past the one everyone else seems to be having. It's a world where, for you, exercise is about physical and mental fitness, not the number on a scale or the shape of your body. It's where food is fuel for energy, not fuel for guilt and punishment. A place where clothes are a form of self-expression rather than a symbol of your goal weight. Imagine how freeing that would be. This book will help you to create that world within yourself.

The book is broken up into three parts: Looking Inward, Looking Outward, and, finally, Onward and Upward.

In Part One, Looking Inward, we'll talk about how much time and brain space we waste thinking negative thoughts about ourselves. Next, we'll brainstorm all sorts of more fun ways to spend that time and energy. We'll reflect on early memories of being told our body wasn't right; meet our "mascots"—who knew all along that this "not right" crap was bullshit; and learn to tune in to internal monologues so we can start being kinder to ourselves. Something to know and highlight: I frequently use "she" to refer to your inner child, but if you prefer something else, please swap in whatever pronoun or word best speaks to you. And, by the way, this book is not only for women: read it out loud and/ or pass it on to any person who could benefit from it.

In Part Two, Looking Outward, we'll learn to take action against the external and internal forces that make us feel ashamed about our body: all the junk we see on TV, the well-meaning yet hurtful comments from our loved ones. We'll talk about shame a lot throughout this book and get really good at giving it the finger. Feel free to give it a go right now! (And by the way, I do curse a lot throughout, so if you prefer to keep your money instead of donating it to the swear jar, replace my F-bombs and S-songs with your version of verbal catharsis.)

By Part Three, Looking Forward, I am confident that you will be able to recognize the power that's always resided within you. Here, we will figure out what to DO with it, which is super fun because I'll basically act like the Cool Grandparent and say "WHATEVER YOU WANT!"

Use this book however works best for you.

You do not have to read it front to back if you'd rather not, though most of the stuff will make more sense if you read it chronologically, like learning a dance routine. It is meant to fit in with the cadence of your life. Pick it up, put it down, let it collect dust and junk mail when you're busy and can't deal. If you're the kind of person who reads magazines back to front, go for it. If you only have time to read one chapter, that's okay! If you only have time to read one sidebar because you're reading this on your phone and you're busy AF and are fitting this in when you pee, that's your truth. Want to read it upside down? Cool (and can you teach me how?). I promise: There is no. Wrong. Way. To read or "do" this book. If you're currently holding it between your hands, reading this page, you're already doing it. One more thing: There are homework assignments throughout this book, but it's entirely up to you when you work on them. I promise: This is the kind of homework you're actually going to use in life.

When you finish this book, pass the message on and move forward with your life.

When yo
this book
the mess
and mov
with you

u finish

pass

age on

forward

life.

LOOKING

IN WARD

(Like, into Your SOUL)

Chapter One

Should I, or Should I Not, Eat This Cookie?

You know what makes me mad? Like just super, super pissed off?

The AMOUNT OF TIME I have wasted thinking NEGATIVE THOUGHTS about my body.

I would estimate that I have spent about . . .

Six million hours feeling like all I wanted to do was shrink myself down and make myself disappear.

Eight hundred fifty years thinking about how much exercising I had to do in order to cancel out calories consumed.

Twenty-three thousand hours wishing I had someone else's arms/legs/stomach/boobs/butt/hands/height/chin.

Forty-six thousand hours using various forms of torture trying to *achieve* said arms/legs/stomach/butt/chin, etc.

About a bajillion minutes worrying what people said about me behind my back—including what they said about how my back actually looked in that dress.

Ten hundred thirty million minutes hating myself when I skipped various forms of torture to do something that sounded way more fun (which of course turned out to be the opposite of fun, because I spent the whole time feeling guilty for skipping said torture).

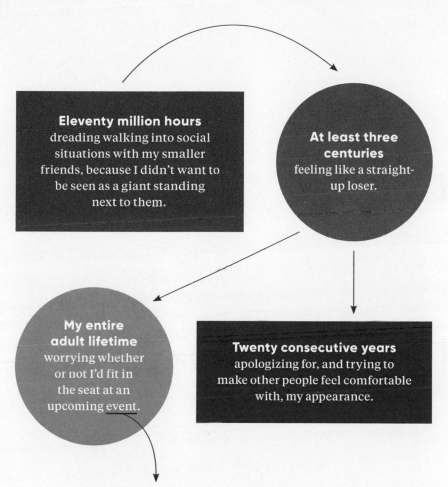

Eleventy million hours dreading walking into social situations with my smaller friends, because I didn't want to be seen as a giant standing next to them.

At least three centuries feeling like a straight-up loser.

My entire adult lifetime worrying whether or not I'd fit in the seat at an upcoming event.

Twenty consecutive years apologizing for, and trying to make other people feel comfortable with, my appearance.

When I say "event," I mean at the movie theater, on a roller coaster, on airplanes, at the dentist, in meetings, at tiny trendy restaurants, at any and every restaurant with communal seating, and—less relatable, I know, but—during fashion week (the seats are teeny-tiny), in the studio where I record *Boob Sweat*, my podcast (I've gotten stuck in those chairs before), in broom-closet-size bathrooms, at my friends' houses . . . of all the lists in this book, this one could go on the longest.

Can you imagine what I could have done with all those hours and days and months and years and centuries spent on body hang-ups? I could have learned how to make flowers out of fondant for wedding cakes, or I could have joined the CIA and put my super facial recognition skills to good use. At the very least, I could have focused more of my attention on the things I valued and enjoyed but never seemed to have enough quality time for—like my friendships, family, career, or traveling (not to sound like a 2011 dating app bio, but). Instead, I exerted all of my time and energy on a never-ending list of things I was convinced were wrong with me.

- **Because of my body, I genuinely felt I would never be successful as a working professional in the fashion industry.**

  "You're too fat," I told myself. Not only did I know I would never fit into the clothes, or even the shoes, I suspected that I'd never fit in with my colleagues and into their physical ideals. (Definitely wasn't gonna fit into their tiny desk chairs.)

- **Because of my body, I never wanted to go dancing with my girlfriends.**

  "You're too much." I didn't want to fill the entire dance floor with my height and my width and my voice and my wingspan.

- **Because of my body, I avoided yoga classes, boxing classes, and Spin classes.**

  "You're too big." Too big to be there, to be seen sweating, to be seen struggling. Too big to be welcome in a space meant for tiny people with god-knows-how-many abs.

But I am here today to tell you that none of it was true.

NONE
of it.

It took a long time for me to realize this. It took even longer for the realization to sink in. I was still talking shit to myself behind my own back when I started The 12ish Style. At the time, I was in a weird place in my first marriage, which would eventually end in divorce. I was in a weird place in my career, which was no longer fulfilling me the way it had been. And I was in an extremely weird place with my body—in part *because of* my marriage and my industry, but also because old body-bashing habits die hard. Ultimately, it was the words of other women—blog and Instagram

comments from women who related to me, and to whom I related—that encouraged me to work through the beef* between me and my body.

<u>I started by paying attention.</u> I already knew I gave myself a hard time, but I didn't realize how *often* I did so—or how harsh it really was—until I started tracking my thoughts. Paying attention forced me to hear my complaints: all of my "Ugh, I feel so fat today" whines, my declarations that "I look like a whale," my promises "to lose twenty pounds before [insert arbitrary season/event/vacation here]."

Noticing these asinine thoughts made me realize how deeply consumed I'd been by them for *my whole life,* and *that* realization made me think about everything I could have done with that whole life had I not spent so much time worrying about whether or not I was too damn big. It took me a while to get there, but I'll never forget the exact moment when, after listening to two interesting, charming women whom I love dearly spend an entire meal complaining about how much weight they'd gained over the holidays, I found myself just . . . totally bored with the conversation.

---

* I should say, "to keep working through the beef," because a big shift like the one we're working through in this book doesn't just happen overnight.

GO FOR THE GOLD
OR GO HOME

(. . . GUESS WHICH ONE I CHOSE)

I should have gone to the Olympics. It's not a guarantee, but when I was in high school, I tested in the 99th percentile for upper-body strength. My dad heard about this and immediately said, "You need to start throwing shot put." Yes, SHOT PUT! Just what every fifteen-year-old girl wants to hear when all she desperately wants is to be dainty. I was already deeply involved in volleyball (which was an acceptable sport in my high school if you wanted to be considered hot at some point), but my dad would not hear my bullshit. "You have a gift," he said. "You must explore it." And so one day, after school, I joined the men's track and field team for a sixty-minute practice to try it. There I was, with my guy friends and crushes, trying to act cute and delicate while simultaneously being taught how to hurl a steel ball from the base of my neck.

Now. I promised that this was a one-time humiliation for me. There was no fucking way I was going to be doing this ever again. I wanted to be a teeny-tiny "girly-girl" who didn't even sweat at volleyball practice. So I quit.

BUT CAN YOU IMAGINE THAT IF I WEREN'T ASHAMED OF MY BODY, I COULD HAVE MAYBE MADE IT TO THE ATHENS 2004 SUMMER OLYMPICS!? I was robbed. By me.

"I was robbed. By me."

And I didn't want to be bored, or boring. I wanted to be great. I wanted to be big! I wanted to be successful and powerful. I wanted to make a difference. I wanted to spend more time doing, trying, helping, living—like, really living—and less time worrying about what my body looked like while *being*.

Imagine how much shit we'd get done if we didn't spend 50 percent of our day agonizing over the cake we did or did not eat at the office birthday. Imagine how much more powerful we'd be if we didn't let the word "FAT" take us down (we'll talk more about that word, by the way, but if you want to talk about it now, check out chapters two and three). Imagine how many more hobbies we'd explore, risks we'd take, and new experiences we'd try if we didn't get bogged down by the anxiety of all that's supposedly "wrong" with us.

Me to Me.

Negative self-talk is loud. It's so loud that it mutes our feelings and desires. The reason we don't always hear ourselves saying these mean things is that we get used to the constant roar. When we start paying attention to how *much* we shit-talk ourselves, however, we can hear the noise for what it is: bothersome, disruptive garbage. And because it's so annoying, so distracting, <u>it's not long before we turn down the blaring radio in our head and say,</u>

"Shut the fuck up. I can't hear my best self think."

Once the noise is gone, it's a whole lot easier to hear yourself whispering about what you really want out of life.

It doesn't matter if your thing is your belly, your nose, your teeth, or your elbow skin: the day you learn how to stop wasting your time on your self-identified or so-called imperfections is the day you'll suddenly have an extra hour to put toward your happiness.

Negative self-talk is LOUD

The next time you're waiting in line at the market or for the bathroom, or when you're sitting in traffic, try adding up how much time you spend, on average, agonizing over the food you did or didn't eat; the clothes that no longer fit or never will; the body parts that jiggle, dimple, wiggle, sway; the hair you don't want versus the hair you wish you had; your height; your foot shape.

Keep adding it all up in your head until you can no longer keep track of the math. And when that happens, ask yourself this: What could you do with all that time instead? What do you *want* to do?

Write down the first five things that come to mind. Or write ten or twelve or a billion if you have them. Let them be weird and fantastical ("I want to become a Yeti preservationist"). Let them be mind-blowingly regular ("I want to read more"). Let them be ambitious ("I want to go back to graduate school"). Let them be leisurely ("I want to take more bubble baths"). The most important part of this exercise is to collect these daydreams and keep them somewhere safe. Write them down in your phone's notes app, draw them in a journal, leave yourself voicemails—just record them in some way, so you can return to them, check in on them, expand upon them, maybe add a few reasonable deadlines, and ultimately, start to *do* some of them.

Chapter Two

Meet Your Mascot

When was the first time you felt that your body was not right?

Take a moment to think about this. Here is your space to pause and reflect.

Scribble all over this page if you find yourself thinking about it and getting sad or angry.

When you're ready to come back, I'll share my experience. The healing comes next.

I was seven years old when I realized my body was "wrong." My mom brought me to the doctor for my annual pediatric checkup—kid stuff—and he put me on a diet. I was a pretty athletic kid. I did all the same physical activities as my sister and my friends, ate what my family ate. I was just . . . bigger than the other kids. Which is something I'd always known! As the only five-foot-six kid in second grade, it wasn't hard to see. But this was the first time I was made to feel ashamed about the bigness of my body.

It wouldn't be the last. I wrote about some of the most impactful moments in the intro (see page 8), and others are sprinkled throughout this book, but here are some major headlines:

@—— ✔

Elderly female neighbor comments on ten-year-old Katie Sturino's "Developing Figure," Katie has no clue what she's supposed to do with that information

2:25 PM • ——— • ———

Why Nine-Year-Old Katie Sturino Wears Her Soccer Coach's Jersey:

"Uh. I don't fit into the kids' jerseys?"

GRAMMAR-SCHOOLER KATIE STURINO REQUIRED TO RUN A LAP FOR EVERY PANCAKE SHE ATE

So That Her Aunt Wouldn't Be Resopnsible for Katie's Additional Weight Gain

Gymnastics Coach Tells Five-Year-Old Aspiring Gymnast Katie Sturino That She's "Too Big for the Sport"

Oh Great: Ogre,

the Nickname Katie Sturino's Friends Gave Her in Middle School, Isn't So Great

Some of these instances seemed straight-up insane to me at the time. Others felt insignificant in the moment and didn't strike me as anything other than "normal." Looking back as an adult, I see how each one built on top of the others throughout my life (not to be dramatic!), adding layers and layers of confirmation to my inner monologue that something was inherently wrong with me because of my size.

Recently, I started thinking more about that diet I was put on in second grade. It is batshit crazy to make a little kid obsess over her calorie intake. I was taught to assign "good" and "bad" values to food and body types before I was old enough to even understand what that meant.

Encourage kids to nourish their bodies with healthy foods, yes. Teach them to eat their vegetables before dessert, to eat less "junk," to move in ways that bring them joy, to play outdoors, to watch less television, to use more of their imagination, and to run around on the playground and shriek with laughter, absolutely. But to tell a child that something is wrong with her body—that the only way to make it right is to restrict food (which is especially confusing when most of your peers are being applauded for finishing their entire lunch)—is just messed up.

I don't have a child of my own, so I don't know what it's like to be told by a medical professional, "Your kid is fat. She has to go on a diet." My mom was doing what she thought was right. She was

SILLY DOCTOR, DIETS AREN'T FOR KIDS

I am seven years old in this picture. This is the same year my doctor put me on a diet. I don't *look* very young here, I know. I was big! Still am. (I'm five-foot-eleven, seven inches taller than the average woman in the United States.)

I have always looked "mature for my age." I think part of why people felt so comfortable saying the kind of things to me one would never say to a *little* kid is because I was BIG. I was *never* a little kid in comparison to my peers. "Little" is always sweet, "so cute," something we instinctually want to take care of, whereas "big"—at least when it relates to the female body—is frequently seen as a fault. The fact is—regardless of my weight or height, regardless of what I looked like—I was a child. I still played with sparkly horse toys at this age. I still believed in Santa Claus. There's no reason I should have had to worry about pleasing others by fitting into their narrow definitions of size. Remind yourself that the next time you find a photo of yourself at the age you were when someone first told you your body wasn't right.

listening to my doctor. She was listening to everything *she'd* ever been taught growing up. She was worried about me and wanted me to experience life without all the baggage of the word "fat" that she (a very average-size woman and much smaller than I am) had.

What I *can* tell you is that the negative effects of the dieting mindset followed me for the rest of my life.

So fuck that doctor, really.

When I posted about this second-grade weight loss program on Instagram and asked if anyone else had been prescribed a baby diet, my inbox was flooded with responses. Some themes:

- **Seven-year-olds sitting in weight loss meetings with full-grown adults**
- **Eight-year-olds having their stomach rolls pinched**
- **Middle-schoolers crying about eating certain foods because they didn't want to get fat**
- **Middle-schoolers with eating disorders**
- **The victorious sound of hearing your stomach growl**
- **Being congratulated by other women (often within the family) for turning food down**

I figured a few women might relate, but I had no idea that SO many of us were holding on to painful memories from childhood that, regardless of specifics, can only be categorized as "The First Time I Remember Being Told There Was Something Wrong with My Body."

If your chest is starting to tighten or your jaw is tensing up because your version of these memories is starting to hit you—the time a fellow first-grader pointed out that you look different from everyone else in the room; the time your crush made fun of your arm hair at a pool party; when the class clown used your acne as a punch line in the middle-school talent show—take a big ol' moment to breathe. Pretend you're in a yoga class and give me a deeeeeeeep inhale, followed by an even deeper exhale. <u>Repeat. Repeat. Repeat.</u>

You're OKAY. You are

BETTER than okay. You're GOOD. You're GREAT.

I'm gonna say what all of us already know: These memories don't have to live at the forefront of our minds to have a lasting negative impact on our self-esteem. They are often buried deep down in the pores of our souls and make themselves known at inconvenient moments. And while we can't change the past, we can absolutely defeat our inner bullies—the voices that reaffirm the shitty messages we first began to internalize as little kids.

And guess what? It's the little kid inside of you who's going to deliver you some peace about your body. <u>That little kid is gonna act as your mascot through this journey.</u>

A SELF-PORTRAIT OF SORTS

I know we just did a whole breathing thing, but let's take another moment to pause here. Grab a snack or run to the bathroom. If you want to bring this book to the bathroom with you, cool. What an honor. If you bring this book with you into the bathroom and then decide, while in there, that you're exhausted from all this internal work and need to take a break and climb into the bath, lovely. Do what you need to do. But when you are ready, start picturing who you were BEFORE society told you that something— or everything—about your appearance was inherently wrong.

Ask yourself these questions: How old were you? What did you look like? What activities do you remember loving? What was your favorite outfit? How did you wear your hair? What was your favorite thing to learn about? Did you have superhero Band-Aids and temporary tattoos all over your arms and legs? When you played make-believe, what did you make-believe about?

Create a mental image of this younger you and keep bringing her into sharper focus. Draw her, if you can. (Use the opposite page!) If you can't draw, scribble. Use her favorite color. Add a superhero cape or a crown, if that's her thing. And if you can't *remember* a time when you weren't "too [enter internalized flaw here]," try to remember a time as a child when you felt your most happy, or a time you were strong, or a time you were brave. (Actually brave, not woman-who-isn't-a-size-0-wears-bikini-on-beach brave. Join me in complaining about how annoying this word can be on page 134.)

This version of you, age ____, is going to become your mascot. This is the you whose inherent confidence and self-esteem radiated through her everyday life, and she's going to help guide you through the healing process. You're going to help her, too. You're going to be kind to her and wrap her with a fleece-lined, weighted empathy blanket should she find some of these exercises challenging. Together, you're going to coax each other to come out of hiding. This isn't the kind of book where the end reveals that the magic has been inside you all along. If you were hoping it was, spoiler alert: We're starting with that information. You *know* there's magic swirling all inside your body and your brain. This book is just here to help you realize it and take back control. We're going to learn how to put an end to the self-shit-talking,* how to relieve ourselves of body shame, how to flip the script of external negative forces, and how to deal with loved ones who say some pretty hurtful things. We are going to learn how to accept our bodies and, with them, all the things we used to consider flaws. We are going to realize the power that's already inside us, learn how to harness it, and then we're going to take action.

Now consult your mascot to confirm that you're both ready to keep moving forward.

---

* You're allowed to curse in front of your inner child so long as it's not about yourself.

DRAW YOUR MASCOT HERE

Chapter Three

You Shut Your Mouth When You're Talking to Me

Allow me to make the mascot thing a little more meta than it already is: Your mascot is here to champion you throughout this process and remind you of the confidence that lives deep within you. But she's also a kid. She's *you* as a kid, remember? <u>And since you're the adult, you have to take care of her.</u>

The FIRST STEP in taking care of your mascot (i.e., yourself) is ending the cycle of BODY SHIT-TALKING

by realizing how we talk to ourselves.

I have been a real asshole to myself over the years, but nothing set me off on a self-shit-talking spiral more than when I felt physically inferior to other women.

In my twenties, before I started the whole internet job situation, I had my own boutique public relations firm that focused on women-owned accessory brands. I loved it: the people I got to work with, the hustling, the strategizing. I especially loved helping and watching female-owned businesses and their founders thrive.

A big part of my job was conducting what we ~in the biz~ call "desksides." A deskside is a meeting in which a publicist brings her client and/or her client's products to her press contacts at their, yup, desks. Visiting the offices of the glamorous magazines I grew up reading should have been thrilling. Instead, it became the most dreaded part of my job because of how it made me feel: Like a failure. Phony. Unsuccessful. Uncool. The fashion industry is a historically exclusive club, one that has long been called out for its lack of inclusivity, not only regarding size and body-type

"I felt like a bear who had accidentally wandered into
the office in a pair of poop-stained sweatpants."

diversity, but also racial diversity and diversity of ability, religion, sexual orientation, and gender representation. While there's still A LOT of work to be done today, let me tell you: Ten or fifteen years ago—whoa, baby, the work had barely begun.

Many of the women I went to visit at these magazines were tall like me, sure. But they were also about half my weight. I always felt Way Too Big, and this was when I was at my most militant about working out and restricting calories (I get into this a bit more on page 157). They were all so beautiful, and they all seemed to have tiny doll feet slipped into sky-high heels, and they all wore the kind of clothes I lusted after but knew I couldn't fit into. No matter what I did when I got dressed those mornings— clothes, hair, makeup—and, more important, no matter how professionally I presented my clients, I never felt like I was supposed to be there. Remember when I told you I felt like a bear in a tutu? At desksides, I didn't even have the tutu: I felt like a bear who had accidentally wandered into the office in a pair of poop-stained sweatpants.

I would say horrible things to myself about how I didn't deserve to be there; how I didn't belong; how I was ugly and unworthy and gross.

turn the page for a list of the horrible things

HORRIBLE THINGS I'VE SAID TO MYSELF

You're a loser, Katie.

You will never be successful.

Who do you think you are? You're not a six-foot-tall blond girl. You can't pull off a casual "jeans and white tee" look! You can't even wear JEANS!

Why did you think you could cut it in New York City? You're not good enough! Look around, and then go back to Wisconsin.

No one's ever going to fall in love with you if you weigh this much.

You're so dumb.

No one will ever describe you as "a natural beauty" or "so elegant."

Was that a joke you just told? Just shut up and stop trying!

You will never be good enough, period.

If first impressions are everything, what the hell do you think yours is saying?

Can't you just be normal??

Why do you always make such weird faces in pictures? Just look normal.

I bet everyone is either hanging out without you, laughing at you, or mad at you purely for existing.

You will never be as good as these women.

Do you know how hard it is to conduct a critical meeting on behalf of a client to sell the fantasy of their newest jewelry line when you're berating yourself?

Actually, I bet you do. Because we all have our own versions of this experience.

The mean things I'd say to myself at these meetings didn't appear in my head out of nowhere. I had, wittingly or unwittingly, learned the basic principles of this practice as I grew up. The older I got, the more fluent I became, until English was my second language. Self-Shit-Talking was my first.

Fat Free ≠ Problems Free

That seemingly carefree girl whose life must be *perfect* because she's a size 2, the girl you bet everyone is in love with: I guarantee her life isn't as perfect as you think. That she's able to wear trendy denim shorts without having her leg circulation cut off does not mean that she doesn't have problems. (Or maybe it does, and she doesn't. What do I know?) I do know this: Losing *or* gaining weight solely to appease societal standards won't magically solve your problems. Problems are problems whether you weigh as much as me or as much as a flea. But you know who has the brains and the wit and the strength to chip away at her problems, work toward her goals, and make her own life a little sunnier? You do, my friend. Also, all those things you want? They're yours for the taking, just as you are, this instant.

It wasn't until I started The 12ish Style that I realized how often I said these kinds of negative things about myself to myself. Of course, this realization didn't solve the problem overnight, but it illuminated all sorts of patterns. I learned to recognize what kinds of situations and interactions made me feel bad about myself. I started realizing who in my life made me feel inferior, what kinds of messages I had internalized as a child, what kinds of messages I was *still* internalizing as an adult, and how all of the above affected my self-esteem, often without me even realizing it. Tracking these patterns crystallized them for me and, ultimately, allowed me to prepare multiple plans of action. It also made me think: <u>Holy shit, Katie. You really gotta be nicer to yourself.</u>

I realized I had been torturing myself for no reason. I thought that if I just showed enough discipline around cheese plates and cut bread out of my diet, if I spent a gajillion dollars on expensive workouts and hours on cardio, then my dream job, dream romantic partner, dream opportunities, and dream life would appear. But weight loss isn't some magic potion that fixes all your problems. I am a hundred pounds heavier now than I was before I started The 12ish Style, and I'm finally genuinely happy. I am confident in myself, in my business, in my extremely loving relationship, and

goal weight

=

+

+

+

Holy shit

You reall

nicer to

Katie.

gotta be
yourself.

in my friendships. The weight gain didn't make these things happen, either, mind you. A change in appearance isn't what sets your life in positive motion. That all those things happened in tandem was more likely a phenomenon tethered to my newfound sense of self-esteem—which of course led me to take more control over my life and go after the things I set my sights on.

Once I started keeping track of all the awful things I said to myself, I noticed that one word stood out:

"FAT."
I wasn't using it merely to

DESCRIBE myself, I recognized. I was using it to INSULT myself.

I knew that "fat" as an insult was something I'd grown up with over the years: Whether from watching TV, reading magazines, hearing what kids said about me on the playground, listening to the women I looked up to as they spoke among themselves,

I
am
fat.
It's okay.
You can
say it.

or likely all of the above, my fear of the word "fat" ran deep. All sorts of external forces had taught me that being fat meant I was obnoxious, undesirable, a joke, unhealthy, and less-than. Perhaps worst of all, I had taught *myself* to associate the word "fat" with being unlovable. I had long feared that no one could possibly love me because of my body type, and since my body type was "fat," that meant my doomed unlovability was all fat's fault. When others called me fat, what I heard was "No one wants you. No one loves you. No one will want or love you." To be fat was to be at once not enough and way, way too much. In my mind, it was the worst thing a person could be, and I was it. I was fat.

I *am* fat. It's okay. You can say it. I can say it. Once I learned, and then finally accepted, that I was inherently, unconditionally worthy of love—and that this love and worthiness has nothing to do with my appearance and/or body, but rather by pure virtue of being a human being—the word "fat" lost its power as an insult. I'm fat? So what! Throw a party for me if you care so much.

Are there words that I prefer over "fat"? Yes, because "fat" can still, on occasion—particularly when I'm feeling low, anxious, insecure—send me careening back into that time on the playground when a boy called me "fat" to be mean. Anytime I run into someone from my past who doesn't know me as the Katie I am so proud to be now, I immediately shrink back into my old, fearful self, and I worry what they will think about my fat. (Then I worry they will text a whole group from my past and tell *them* how

85

THE MANTRA

You, too, are inherently worthy of love. We're gonna repeat that over
and over together in a bit. It'll be fun, I think. If we can accept that
our appearance (including weight and body type) isn't the thing that
makes us lovable, successful, fun, stylish, etc., then we can accept
our weight as our weight, our appearance as our appearance. Nothing
more, nothing less. It just *is*. It's one thing to say it, I know, and quite
another to believe it. So for now, think of "I am inherently worthy of love"
as a mantra to repeat until your believing it becomes second nature.

**You are
inherently
worthy of
love.**

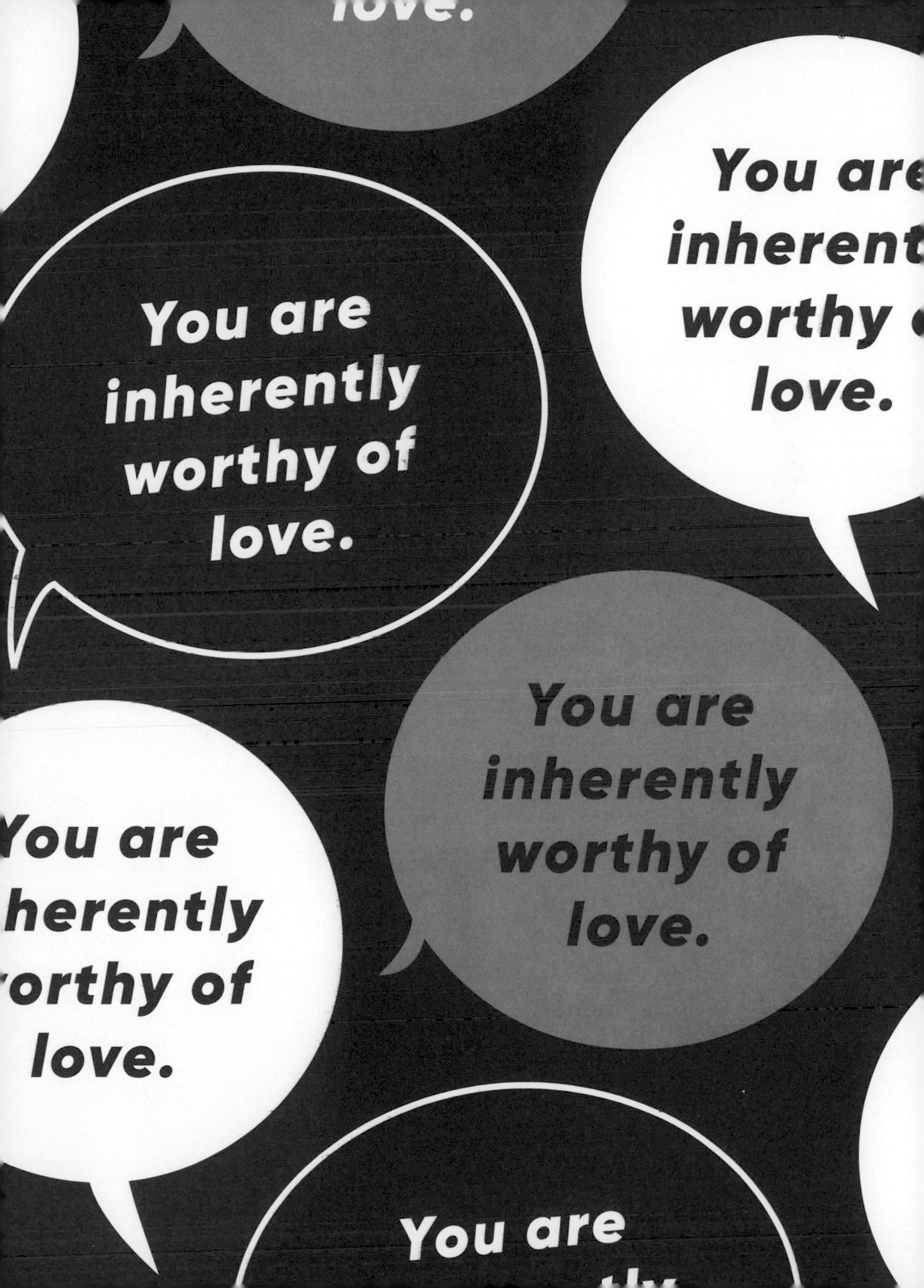
You are inherently worthy of love.
You are inherent worthy love.
You are inherently worthy of love.
You are herently orthy of love.
You are

fat I've gotten, and that it must be because of something pathetic.) "Fat" is still the first insult I throw at myself, because it was the first insult I learned to throw at myself. But now I catch myself doing it, and I challenge "fat" as an insult. After all, it can't be an insult if I don't choose to take it as one.

It's possible the word "FAT" doesn't make you blink.

It's possible you're like, "What's the big deal?" It's possible you took back this word long ago from the external forces that tried to use it against you and now you wear "fat" like a badge of pride, in which case, pass that sentiment *on*! Yes! This is what I'm talking about. We all could use more of this thinking. But know this: When it comes to our appearance, we're all insecure about *something*, and that insecurity is rooted in fear.

Shout-out
to the women in the
body positivity community
who have reclaimed the word
"fat" and turned it into something
worth celebrating. The way they've
stripped "fat" of its shame and
infused it with joy has helped my
own relationshipwith the word,
and with the fat on my
body, immensely.

Let's pause here. I'd like you to think about some of your body-centric insecurities and their associated scary words. Then dig deep:

What is your greatest fear about these insecurities being true?

If you can stand it, I encourage you write this down.

Next, let's write out a quick reminder to be nicer to ourselves.

Holy shit, _____.
[write your name here!]

You gotta be nicer to yourself.

Love,

_____
[Your name here again]

I fully support you ripping that reminder out of this book and taping it to your mirror, by the way.

WRITE YOUR INSECURITIES AND SCARY WORDS HERE

Now that you've written out a reminder, take this week to pay attention to the way you talk to yourself. You don't have to DO anything with that information yet, but start keeping track of all the times you bash yourself. If you have one of those brains where you can just store and recall information willy-nilly, great. If you're better off writing things down when they come to mind, keep a notebook with you or use your phone.

As you start paying closer attention to your internal negative scripts, start asking yourself if you notice any Mean Themes emerging. Some common ones:

Not being "enough" (not good enough, smart enough, pretty enough).

Being too much (too big, too short, too weird).

Maybe your shit-talking focuses on specific, self-designated flaws: your "problem areas."

Maybe it's a whole lot of self-blame and self-shaming: "It's your fault your _____ looks like _____ because _____." (Subtext: You're a monster, self.)

You may frequently find yourself imagining the better life you'd have *if only* it weren't for your [insert "flaw"/ "flaws"].

Or your self-shit-talking theme may center around a key word (kinda like mine did): Ugly. Dumb. Stupid. Unworthy. Weird. Freak. Bad.

I'm gonna leave a little space on the next page for you to keep track of the Mean Themes as they start to pop up. I know it's scary to face them, but as is the case when puking up toxic bile (sorry), better out than in.

Look at what you wrote down. Now yell the following at them:

YOU HOLD NO POWER OVER ME!

Again!

YOU HOLD NO POWER OVER ME!

LOUDER! (It's fine. Your neighbor will think you're watching a movie.)

YOU HOLD NO POWER OVER ME!

If you can't bring yourself to yell out loud, for now just yell in your head. But do try to find a place where you can yell this—the shower with music blasting? an empty field?—because I promise you, it's cathartic.

When you're done yelling, try this: Find a pen and draw little happy doodles all over those so-called scary words. Give your insecurity and your fear each a tail. What about ears? Make them meow! Add anything you need to those words to make them less scary.

Now, the next time any of these insecurities and fears and scary words pop into your head, I want you to tell them what you already know: "YOU HOLD NO POWER OVER ME!"

You hear that whooping? That's your mascot cheering for you.

WRITE YOUR MEAN THEMES HERE

You hold NO POWER over me!

Chapter Four

It's as Easy as N-O-P-E.

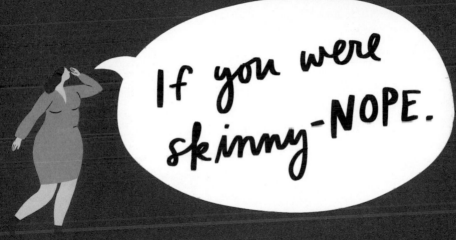

Now that we are aware of how we're talking to ourselves, let's learn how to *stop talking shit*.

The first time a photo shoot featuring me instead of my dog was published on a public forum,* I was surprised to find that the comments were filled with excitement and enthusiasm. I didn't disgust the entire internet with my being, as I had originally worried I would. Instead, I was overwhelmed with kindness from women who were excited to see my body type—*their* body type—wearing clothes they'd assumed they couldn't "pull off." They wanted to know where I found shoes for my size 12 feet, they wanted to know the brand of my leather jacket, and they wanted to see even more of me, if you can believe it. I couldn't.

Their positivity sparked a little something-something in my brain.

"Is it possible," I began to wonder,

---

* On a fashion blog that I used to read for outfit inspiration, no less, whose style suggestions I never thought I could pull off, until I did. (Check out the introduction, starting on page 8, for the whole story if you skipped it and are now like, "Huh??")

"that there isn't ANYTHING wrong with my size or shape?"

And that question, though hypothetical* at the time, started the chain reaction that led to the next phase of my life. Affirmations from other women continued as I began to wade deeper and deeper into the pool party of body acceptance and positivity. Women told me in person and on Instagram about the shorts they finally wore that they never thought they could, about the bikini pictures they were finally posting after a lifetime of not feeling

---

* Hypothetical because the automatic answer in my brain was still "Hahahahah wait hahahahah Katie hahahah oh god, that's too good, of course there's something wrong with your size and shape! Gross!"

"beach body ready." Their confidence made it impossible to *not* pay attention to the Mean Things I was still saying to myself (see page 76 if you're bouncing around). The contrast was stark—and then one day, I had enough. So I stopped.

OKAY . . . I feel like I can *hear* you yelling at me through the pages:

"OH YEAH, SURE, KATIE, YOU JUST STOPPED? IT WAS THAT EASY, HUH?"

Well, not exactly, because learning to pay attention to and keep track of your negative thoughts is hard. It's the opposite of fun. But guess what? If you've read chapter three, you're already well on your way.

How to Stop Shit-Talking Yourself

- **Step 1:** Pay attention to the shit-talking (again, see chapter three).

- **Step 2:** Scare your Mean Themes and scary words by telling them "You hold no power over me!"

- **Step 3:** Your negative thoughts will become less aggressive after Step 2, but, guaranteed, they will still appear. Sometimes new ones pop up out of nowhere! Don't freak out when this happens. Just yell "NOPE!" at them inside your brain.

- **Step 4:** Replace every negative thought with a positive thought.

  That's kinda it. But don't worry. I'm gonna coach you through it . . .

How to "NOPE"

Stand in front of the biggest, tallest mirror you can find. The goal is to get the fullest possible picture of yourself.

Now observe: How do you receive yourself in the mirror?

You may find yourself immediately drawn to all the flaws. You may notice new so-called flaws. You may add even *more* items to your never-ending "to improve" list. Whatever's going on in that

brain of yours, channel your inner mascot, put your hands on your hips, and say a firm and clear NOPE!

<u>The goal is to shut down that shit-talking before it can even begin.</u>

- "Hey stomach, why are you so—" **NOPE!**
- "Hey nose, you stin—" **NOPE!**
- "Hey acne, you are ruining my—" **NOPE!**

Nope, nope, nope. Just NOPE! Like you're telling a toddler that touching a hot oven is not a good idea.

I'm not asking you to write a sonnet to your cellulite or to sext yourself photos of your own ass or to propose to your arm jiggle. I'm not asking you to declare your love for your teeth or your boobs or your ears. That wasn't my path. It doesn't need to be yours. Right now, all I'm asking you to do is to block the shit-talk, remove the shame, and, eventually, stop equating your VALUE with these things.

If you're struggling, consider this: Your job is to protect your mascot, right? And she's a child, right? Rule of thumb: If you wouldn't let someone say it to your sweet and mighty mascot, who is a CHILD, don't say it to yourself!

Homework assignment

№ 4

MANDATORY NAP TIME

Speaking of child, your mascot could probably use an emotional nap right about now. Put the book down, even if it's for five minutes, close your eyes, and take a break. (Looking at your phone does not count as a break!)

Practice Makes No-Such-Thing-as-Perfect

Once you've got your NOPEs down—not perfected, just down, as in you can get the nope out of your mouth, or into your head, or at the very least you're on board with the concept—I'm gonna need you to head back to that mirror.

This time, you're gonna follow up your NOPEs with compliments. The compliments don't have to be related to what you're NOPE-ing right now—they just have to be about you. EVERYONE has something on their body and in their brain that's exceptional.

So here's how that would look:

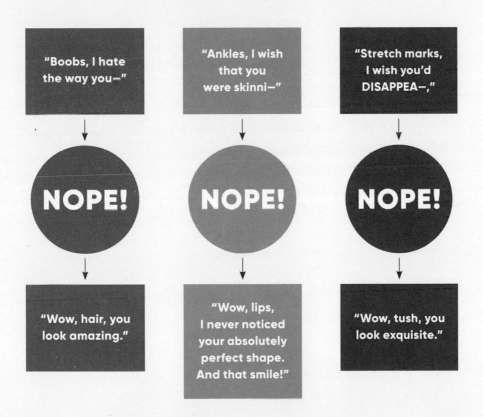

"Boobs, I hate the way you—"

"Ankles, I wish that you were skinni—"

"Stretch marks, I wish you'd DISAPPEA—,"

NOPE!

NOPE!

NOPE!

"Wow, hair, you look amazing."

"Wow, lips, I never noticed your absolutely perfect shape. And that smile!"

"Wow, tush, you look exquisite."

Got it? Now off you go to practice!

That Douche SHAME

<u>What you should know about Shame is that Shame's a real asshole.</u> Doesn't Shame even *sound* like an asshole name from an '80s movie?

FLASHBACK TO THE '80S

- **Some Random Guy:** "Hey, *Shame*! Killer party last night. What's on for today?"

- **Shame:** "Oh you know, the usual. Make that girl Katie feel bad for existing in her human form. Thought I'd point out that she's the only girl in her grade who has cellulite. Remind her that she's a freak for being taller than all the boys she knows. Make her feel like a monster for wearing her dad's old T-shirt to a sleepover where all her miniature friends will be wearing cutesy unicorn pajamas that don't come in her size. The usual."

SHAME SUCKS!
Feel free to say that out loud right now.

Think about all the stupid, arbitrary restrictions you have previously placed on yourself because of shame of your body. I used to tell myself I couldn't wear shorts because I was too big. I wanted *so badly* to look like my teeny-tiny friends in their teeny-tiny denim cutoffs, but instead, every time I put them on, I felt like a polar bear with a denim wedgie, and I do *not* mean that in a sexy way.

If you have time and energy, use this space to capture three limiting thoughts caused by that asshole Shame:

I can't wear/do _____ because _____.

I can't wear/do _____ because _____.

I can't wear/do _____ because _____.

Now, can you challenge that thought?

I challenge the thought of being unable to wear shorts with "I *can* wear shorts because I can wear whatever I want to wear. I can wear shorts because my legs deserve to breathe* and feel the sun!"

Your turn to try it:

I CAN wear/do _____ because _____.

I CAN wear/do _____ because _____.

I CAN wear/do _____ because _____.

---

* Apologies to my vageen when I sit down, though.

While we're here, let's all take a second to give a big MIDDLE FINGER to Shame.

Tell Shame to **back** **the** **EFF off**

Bird-flip or not, I do still shame myself sometimes. It's not like I've reached some form of body acceptance nirvana. That's . . . not a thing. We all have our bad days, no matter how much progress we make. Even the best potty-trained adults can have accidents! So let's all be a little kinder to ourselves here. If you find yourself falling right back into your old shamey ways, pretend you're a puppy who peed on the floor (I'm writing this while I have to go to the bathroom), shake your head, pat yourself on the butt, clean up the mess, and try again.

I REPEAT: The ultimate goal is not to fall madly in love with your every self-determined flaw.

If you can't stand your feet, I don't expect you to bend over and start making out with them. The goal is stop equating your VALUE with these flaws. Tell Shame to back the EFF off so you can focus on the things you'd rather be doing instead.

Before I began The 12ish Style, I knew I needed *some* sort of change in my life. I did not, however, know what I wanted that change to be. So I started small—about as small as one could start, really.

I started writing a list of things that made me happy, like emotions, experiences, and places. I'd be incredibly embarrassed if anyone ever saw that old list, even now, because it was so cheesy, but also, so what?

One thing I wrote down was a dream I had of owning an ice cream shop. I've dreamed of this forever. I wanted an ice cream shop, and it needed to have a bench outside because I wanted a community to form around this little scoop of dairy heaven. I wanted my ice cream shop and its bench to become a New York City staple, where friends could run into each other or meet up on purpose—a real neighborhood feel.

I ended up starting a fashion blog focused on body acceptance instead. It's not an ice cream shop, but it did introduce me to an incredible community where friends run into each other and meet up on purpose, real neighborhood feel and all.*

The point of writing out your dreams is less about literally manifesting them and more about opening yourself up to the childhood practice of dreaming.

---

* BYO ice cream cone.

"One thing I wrote down was a dream I had
of owning an ice cream shop."

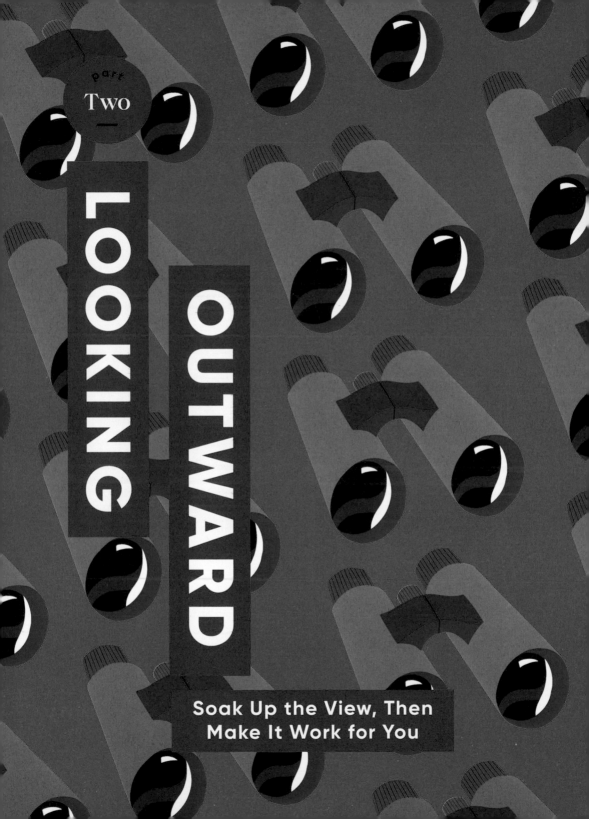

part
Two
—

LOOKING

OUTWARD

Soak Up the View, Then
Make It Work for You

Chapter Five

Cutting Out the Junk Food

Do you know what the unhealthiest thing in your diet is?

- **Cookie dough? Guess again.**

- **Chips? Ha! Sorry, Charlie!**

- **Pizza?! Fuck, no! Pizza is the food of the gods.**

Fine, I'll just tell you:

The WORST thing in your DIET

is all
the
TOXIC
BODY
MESSA-
GING
we are fed.

For example: Fat jokes on prime-time television; weight loss ads on Instagram; billboards for cellulite-removing laser services; magazines featuring tips for getting "better" skin alongside an endless slew of products to fix you—from the hair on your head to the hair on your toes; in movies: prescriptions for the size, shape, and buoyancy of your boobs; in online click-bait articles: stories about women who find love only after they complete a twenty-step makeover that includes a grueling fitness journey and the magical letting-go of past trauma and baggage.

Are you exhausted yet? I don't think we realize how often we're bombarded by negative messaging about our bodies—and this list isn't even exhaustive.

Every time we see ourselves as the undesirable "before" picture in a miraculous transformation; every time we see ourselves as the butt of the joke; every time we *don't* see ourselves among those who are considered "worthy," our mascots pull the covers up higher over their heads.

I want to walk you through a day-in-the-life of the external toxic body messaging that I, personally, am prone to internalize. Let's pretend it's Saturday (and I'm way busier than usual, for the sake of packing a punch, okay?).

turn the page for my day-in-the-life

"Are you exhausted yet?"

A Day-in-the-Life of External Toxic Body Messaging

6:00 a.m.
I'm an early riser by nature, so I'm out the door and on a walk with the dogs. While they poop, I scroll through Instagram. I stop on a sponsored post promoting a so-called stomach-flattening "detox" tea that I'm pretty sure just gives you diarrhea.

6:30 a.m.
I spend half an hour lost in a #beforeandafter rabbit hole thanks to a hashtag under that stupid diarr-tea. The comments about the women's "before" photos are filled with fat jokes and barf emojis. My body looks like many of the "before" bodies. For some reason, I can't stop scrolling. Against my better reasoning, I can't stop reading the comments either.

9:00 a.m.
I go to a workout class where the instructor tells us to push harder if we want to look hot in our bikinis this summer. People still say things like that?

9:05 a.m.
I realize this class has the worst playlist ever.

9:07 a.m.
I seriously can't focus, this music is so bad.

9:15 a.m. I notice that I am, by far, the largest person in the room. I see that a lot at trendy boutique fitness classes, where, despite the cheery, all-in-this-together mentality, it's hard to feel welcome if you don't show up looking like a '90s runway model.

10:00 a.m. On my way out of the class, I stop by a rack of workout clothes in the reception area. Maybe a new outfit will make me feel more '90s-bikini-model-esque. (They got in my head, I can't help it!) I'm sorry to admit that I want it all: the overpriced crop tops and the stupid-expensive workout tights and the limited-edition sweatshirts. Luckily for my credit card, nothing on this rack would fit me.

10:15 a.m. As I leave the studio, I overhear the front desk asking a bride-to-be if she'd like to sign up for their "Shedding for the Wedding" program. She says yes, and I silently thank myself for only buying one class at this place, not a whole package.

11:00 a.m. I meet some friends for brunch and try to ignore the table next to us as two beautiful women bemoan how they're already ruining their diets and It's not even noon.

11:02 a.m. I notice this menu has "skinny" lattes in addition to regular lattes, if you were worried. I was worried.

12:45 p.m. A bus just drove by with an ad featuring a sassy woman savoring a *tiny* piece of dark chocolate. She seems to be letting me in on her size-0 secret: "If you're gonna cheat on your diet, make it count. But, more important, make it small."

1:00 p.m. My friends and I decide to go shopping at this place around the corner that "everyone" has been talking about. "Everyone" finds something to try on except me because they have nothing in my size. A salesperson cheerfully tells me that they do, however, have a pair of black leggings that stretch! I thank her and try on sunglasses.

1:15 p.m. No luck at the next store either.

1:30 p.m. Now we're in a store that tells me to check out their website for larger sizes. I take out my phone and head to the website to kill time while my friends complain from the dressing room about feeling fat after breakfast. There are two styles in my size online and they are so drab I almost think it's a prank. "The most flattering dress you'll ever own," one description promises. The other boasts an "accentuated waist." I feel an eye roll coming. Maybe I should have bought those sunglasses.

3:45 p.m. I show up for a massage my husband got me at a super fancy hotel for my birthday. I've been looking forward to it for months. Upon signing in at reception, I'm handed a luxurious, fluffy robe and directed toward a changing room.

3:50 p.m. I discover this robe was meant for a toddler. I'm full-on tits-out and you can read the day of the week on my underwear—that's how much skin I'm showing. The belt on this thing could be a headband. I don't want to flash my masseuse, so I get dressed and head back out to the front desk.

4:05 p.m. I ask for a new robe and am told that they already gave me the largest men's size possible, but they'll check in the back for an extra towel. I alternate between apologizing profusely and thanking them sincerely.

 4:06 p.m. I wonder if this debacle is cutting into my massage time.

 6:10 p.m. I'm sitting at the movies and can't get comfortable. The seat is so damn small, I'm going to have to make a move on my husband, who's sitting next to me, just so I can get my arm in a more comfortable position. He's having the same problem, though, and I'm reminded why we never come to this theater.

6:13 p.m. A preview comes on for some stupid-but-funny-looking comedy movie that I keep hearing about. There's a lotttttaaa fat jokes.

9:00 p.m. We're home and I get sucked into a trashy TV show featuring a cast of women wearing tight size 00 clothes, vying for the attention of a few pretty unremarkable dudes. Do they all have the same trainer or something? How do they all have the *exact* same body type?

127

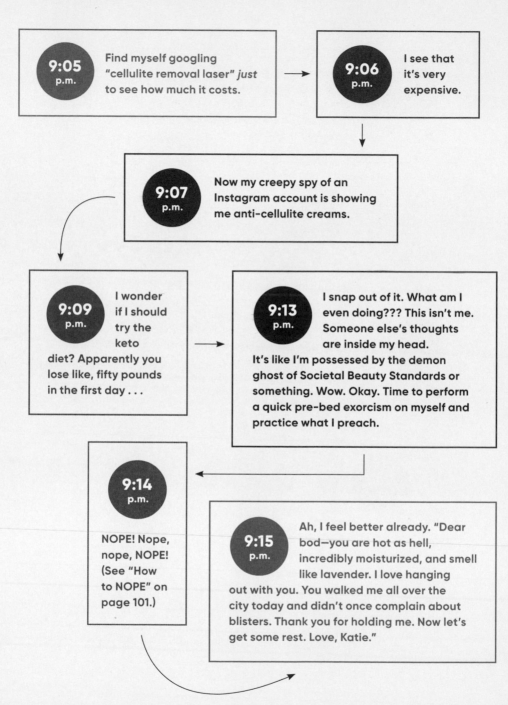

9:05 p.m. Find myself googling "cellulite removal laser" *just* to see how much it costs.

9:06 p.m. I see that it's very expensive.

9:07 p.m. Now my creepy spy of an Instagram account is showing me anti-cellulite creams.

9:09 p.m. I wonder if I should try the keto diet? Apparently you lose like, fifty pounds in the first day . . .

9:13 p.m. I snap out of it. What am I even doing??? This isn't me. Someone else's thoughts are inside my head. It's like I'm possessed by the demon ghost of Societal Beauty Standards or something. Wow. Okay. Time to perform a quick pre-bed exorcism on myself and practice what I preach.

9:14 p.m. NOPE! Nope, nope, NOPE! (See "How to NOPE" on page 101.)

9:15 p.m. Ah, I feel better already. "Dear bod—you are hot as hell, incredibly moisturized, and smell like lavender. I love hanging out with you. You walked me all over the city today and didn't once complain about blisters. Thank you for holding me. Now let's get some rest. Love, Katie."

Raise Your Hand If . . .

Raise your hand if you've apologized for your body before. I'm raising my hands AND my feet because I still find myself doing it every single day. Apologizing for our bodies is as unnecessary as apologizing for breathing. So please repeat after me: *My body is not an imposition. My body is allowed to be here. I am allowed to be here.* (If cursing feels good to you, throw a "fucking" somewhere in that sentence.)

In reading through my day, you might recognize similar external negative forces in your own daily life. (BTW: Let's call external negative forces "ENuFs" from here on out because it's too much of a mouthful otherwise. I stuck the little *u* in there because ENF makes me think of ENuF, as in ENOUGH ALREADY! Cut this shit out!) Maybe you're affected by entirely different ENuFs than the ones I mentioned. We're all different, and beauty standards are SUPER narrow, which means each of us is bound to feel attacked by different ENuFs in different ways. Because of that, I encourage you to familiarize yourself with and to pay close attention to the ENuFs that directly affect your personal confidence. In fact . . .

Right now, we are in the process of UN-learning the "shoulds" of what our bodies "should" look like.

I should have perfect skin. I should be completely hairless, except for the hair on my head, which should look exactly like this famous musician whose picture I've brought to the salon, and when I leave, no matter how much damage is required to get it there, it should feel as healthy as the green smoothie I should be drinking each morning. (After I do some torturous workout, of course, so I can feel as though I earned my breakfast.) I should have little princess feet and perfectly manicured hands at all times. I should have odorless armpits, entirely free of stubble or hair and those little balls of lint that cling to the creases of my armpit skin. I should have designer clothes, expensive shoes, an Instagram-ready outfit on at all times, including while sleeping, and I should look like I didn't try. I should eternally strive to appear effortless. I should wear just enough makeup to make me look "fresh," but not enough so that you can tell I'm wearing makeup—unless I'm attending a fancy event, in which case, I should have mastered the art of the perfect smoky eye. I should have the same body as an airbrushed actress in a photo shoot. I should have the same physical blueprint of a supermodel. I should have a thigh gap. I should have perfectly straight teeth and no bump on my nose. I should have zero wrinkles. I should, I should, I should.

Aren't you exhausted?

You know what's even more exhausting? That with all these *shoulds* comes the underlying implication that we have to punish ourselves (with painful beauty treatments and excessive workouts, by replacing meals with liquid despite our jaws being perfectly capable of chewing) in order to achieve such Should-y goals. Why are we always made to feel like we have to EARN our calories, our "beach bodies," others' stamps of attraction and approval? The next time someone tells you, a full-grown adult who's responsible for her own life, that she has to "earn" a piece of cake before she can actually enjoy it, hold up your middle finger like a birthday candle, blow, and make a wish.

In order to UN-learn all these shoulds, we have to recognize the junk food messaging for what it is: <u>CRAP.</u>

CREATIVE WRITING

Write out your own day-in-the-life-of. Pull from memory, or do it in real time as you go about your day.

As you do it, ask yourself: What ENuFs make regular, unwelcome, pain-in-the-ass appearances? Don't be shy. Don't worry about being "too sensitive." Be honest about the things that bother you, that make you feel crappy. That make you feel less-than. This exercise is best repeated a few times over the course of a week, or a month, or whenever you feel like checking in. Each time you do it, you'll get better at identifying things that you may not even have realized were bothering you. (We'll get the people in your own lives who directly affect your confidence—whether unwittingly or willingly—in chapter 6.)

"Wow, Katie, that sounds like a terrible idea. Probably the worst idea ever. You want me to go around paying particular attention to that which makes me feel like crap? Shouldn't I just ignore this stuff?"

Great question. Because ENuFs are so pervasive and shape-shifty and can affect us differently depending on our mental state on any given day, at any given moment, I'm not so sure I believe that we can "just ignore this stuff." It gets in there without our noticing. So while it may sound like a terrible idea to keep what is ultimately an anti-gratitude list of all the things that make you feel bad, what we're doing is identifying ENuFs so that we can release their grip of power from our brain space. When we know what our daily ENuFs are, we can spot them a mile away, then choose to change direction, or counteract them, or flip them the good ol' bird.

WRITE YOUR DAY-IN-THE-LIFE HERE

I don't thin

realize ho

we're bon

negative n

about our

k we

v often

oarded by

essaging

oodies.

<u>Once we recognize the crap for shit, we can become faster and fiercer at raising our ever-powerful NOPE! flag.</u> Instead of automatically agreeing with critiques, we start to stand up for our self-worth. Defending our mascot becomes a reflex.

Along with identifying our ENuFs and their accompanying shoulds and waving our NOPE flags and saying NOPE out loud, here are some other ways to take charge:

1. We can control our own reaction to ENuFs by flipping the world's most cliché breakup line and turning it into a helpful mantra: "It's not me, it's YOU. And your bullshit." Think of this as mental armor against any and all ENuFs. Try saying it to yourself next time you come across an advertisement that makes you feel like you need to fix something on or about your body. Repeat as often as you need.

2. We can cut out the ENuFs in our physical, daily lives that we have control over cutting out (like, why are you still subscribed to that magazine that makes you feel bad about yourself each month?) and replace them with something positive. (Instead of a magazine that gives you a new extreme diet to try each month, what about buying a magazine that focuses on a hobby you've always wanted to try? Donate your bathroom scale, and treat yourself to a fluffy new bath mat. Look up a different route so that as you drive to the grocery store, you bypass that *obnoxious* billboard and instead drive past a peaceful park.)

3. **Unfollow every single ENuF in your digital world.** I know it's hard to "cut out" content when it feels like it's coming at you from all sides, but unfollowing accounts that make you feel bad is a great step. If you feel yourself worrying about hurting one of these accounts' feelings for unfollowing, ask yourself what's more important: their follower count, or your well-being?

4. **Build boundaries** around the ENuFs you can't avoid or unfollow (for whatever reason, and you know what? I'm sure there are many). For example: "The window of my corner office looks directly out onto a billboard that equates the removal of 'unsightly acne scars' with an inevitable promotion: 'Put your best face forward and get the job of your dreams!' So, I blocked that part of the view with a giant vase of my favorite flowers, and reminded myself that my acne-scarred face and I have a big fancy corner office and a parking spot with our name on it."

5. **Identify where else you can shed ENuFs.** Once you start looking, it'll be like dog hair: everywhere.

As you go about your day this week, try putting some of these tools into action. Think baby steps, and feel free to baby your baby steps, but if your mascot gets bold and is raring to go, lace up her sneakers and let her run with it.

It's totally normal to let something get to you during your body acceptance adventure. You are not failing at this if you re-read a negative script that you used to recite to yourself on autopilot. You aren't going to undo the progress you've been making. If you thought you were past feeling less-than every time you see advertisements of so-called "perfect" women, then find yourself sorely mistaken, take a few deep breaths and remember it's all a process.

You know what else is helpful to remember about the process? It's for YOU. It is ABOUT you.

So make it work for you! Do you feel like things are moving too fast? Slow it down a bit. Having a hard time processing some of the very real, very intense emotions we're working through? Give yourself a foot massage. Is your head swirling because you made an outrageously long list of all the "bad habits" you want to change and now you're overwhelmed? Pause! Take a beat here and reflect: What improvements do YOU want to make for yourself, if any? (P.S. You do not need FIXING! This is about healing. If it feels like an inauthentic, unnecessary makeover task for the sake of appeasing someone else, don't do it!) It helps to ask yourself *why* you want to change or improve each so-called bad habit. If your

It's for
YOU.
It is
ABOUT
you.

LET'S TAKE A MOMENT TO TALK ABOUT HOW ANNOYING THE WORD "BRAVE" CAN BE

When it comes to describing women above a certain size and their naked, or mostly naked, or flamboyantly covered bodies, the word "brave" is bullshit.

Firefighters are brave. People who catch and release spiders are brave. Your mascot is brave. But when I wear a two-piece swimsuit to the hot-AF beach and/or post a picture of myself in that two-piece on the internet, I am not being brave. I'm just doing what feels right and good? I don't know! Why does anyone wear a swimsuit to the beach or post photos of it on the internet? Because they want to???

When people use the word "brave" in this context, it's as though what they're actually saying is "Your body is embarrassing. You *should* be ashamed of it. But because you're not ashamed—even though we're all a little horrified that your ass and flub are out and we would never do such a thing if we were you—well, that takes a lotta guts! (Especially because you, Katie Sturino, have a lotta gut.)"

What about *feeling* brave? Isn't that valid? Of course it is! You might feel *exceptionally* brave the first time you wear something you never thought you could pull off because of your size. That act might make you feel like a straight-up superhero. It's made me feel powerful!

What I ask, dear society, media, men, and whoever else, is that when it comes to our bodies, let each of us as women, as individuals, decide when we are and when we are not being brave. Let us make that call for ourselves.

"When people look at my body and be like, 'Oh my God, she's so brave,' it's like, 'No, I'm not . . . I'm just fine. I'm just me. I'm just sexy.' If you saw Anne Hathaway in a bikini on a billboard, you wouldn't call her brave. I just think there's a double standard when it comes to women."
—LIZZO

"This is where I get really 'brave,' as everyone said after my [naked] Annie Leibovitz photo. . . . That's what you want everyone to say when a naked photo of you goes viral. You want them to say 'What a brave photo.' You're like, 'Thanks, wow, thank you.'"
—AMY SCHUMER

"[P]eople would say 'You're so brave to wear those outfits.' The implicit feeling is *You are ugly. Why do you think you should be able to wear those things?*"
—MINDY KALING

answer ever begins "Because X said I should," that's not reason
enough to waste your energy on it. Even if I or this book said it!
Remember: When it comes to body acceptance and self-esteem,
you are your priority. You are doing this for YOU.

This isn't a sprint. This isn't a marathon, either! You're not being
timed at all. You are not required to check in with anyone except
yourself. There are no registration papers to fill out. There are
no forms to sign. Your inner mascot is a child—she doesn't even
know what paperwork is! (When she finds it lying around, she
naturally assumes it's for her to tear up and use to make confetti.)
I repeat yet again because I can't repeat it enough: You do not
need fixing. You are wonderful and whole as is. You do not need
yet another thing added to your to-do list. This wild ride of a
journey is an elective lazy river that you're welcome to exit and
re-enter with your inner tube as you wish, so long as what you're
doing feels good. If an exercise in here feels like a delicious,
satisfying stretch, keep going. If it feels like you're about to pop
a joint out of its socket, stop. Breathe. Come back when
you're rested and ready.

I want to get real for a minute before we go any further.

Narrow beauty standards very much exist within the world of body positivity

Even as more businesses and brands promise to make bigger steps toward greater inclusivity, there is still a monolithic kind of "aspirational fat" that proliferates, a singular type of woman who gets featured, designed for, photographed, uplifted, and celebrated in the media. She is almost always white, cisgendered, able-bodied, and a size 14. (This is me. Hello. I am clear-eyed about the fact that I have benefited, for sure, from the associated privileges, and it is part of my work to uplift and shout-out to others who do not!) The circumference of this aspirationally fat woman's waist is significantly smaller than her chest and her hips. Her stomach is flat, she *never* has a double chin (I would like to note that I always do), and she is somehow, miraculously, dusted only ever so slightly with a scattering of cellulite and barely there stretch marks. If she has any wrinkles, they're playful little pleats that appear only when she grins or winks.

If this were a drive-through window where I could order anything I wanted, I'd ask for every brand, publication, billboard, and runway to hire, celebrate, feature, and make products for a diverse representation of races, ages, abilities, gender orientations, sexual orientations, and more—*as well as* celebrate different body shapes, weights, and sizes.

Can you help make this a reality? YES! By joining

the BODY POSITIVITY and BODY ACCEPTANCE movement.

The more of us, the better. By calling out brands that refuse to do better and calling *in* brands that you *know* can do better. By calling in friends and family members! By supporting businesses, brands, initiatives, organizations, and platforms owned and led by women of color, differently abled women, Queer women, Trans women, Indigenous women, people who don't identify with the gender binary at all, and women who wear plus sizes, who inherently understand the frustrations of shopping for clothes over a size 12! By supporting female-founded companies who've been inclusive out of the gate. By encouraging the brands that are making real strides toward inclusivity to keep on keeping on. By starting *your* own thing.

#SUPERSIZE
THE LOOK

Lest you think I'm a one-hashtag wonder, I also started a recurring series of Instagram posts called "SuperSize the Look": I post a photo of a celebrity in a cool outfit, and next to them, a shot of me wearing my interpretation of their look. The point is to show that women of *all* sizes can pull off the kind of outfits they're inspired by but tend to assume they can't wear. (Because of ENuFs.)

However, whenever I post a "SuperSize the Look" Instagram, someone invariably comments which of the two women—either myself, or the celebrity inspiration—wore it better. That's the opposite reaction from what I want to inspire. Our society's reflexive habit of pitting women against one another is what contributes to infighting among women. How are we supposed to grow and thrive when we're wasting our energy telling a celebrity on the red carpet that she looks like she's gained fifty pounds since her last movie?

But listen! LISTEN! I understand the urge! Most of us grew up with magazines, tabloids, television programs, and beauty pageants that asked us to choose winners from groups of women in glamorous outfits. We have been programmed to identify the prettiest and best-dressed woman any time there are two or more pictured together. We gobble up photos of stars with acne, cellulite, rolls, postpartum bellies, and everything else that comes with having a human body, because we have been taught that such celebrity sightings are unfathomable rarities. We have been taught *since childhood*—is your mascot paying attention?—that living "happily ever after" pertains not only to finding love (the archaic and FALSE messaging there: Shack up, or be alone and miserable), but, often, to transforming from a pumpkin into a society's narrow beauty ideal: the original before and after.

#MAKEMYSIZE!

One of the biggest ENuFs in my life is the fact that so many clothing brands I love and want to support don't make clothes in my size. It sucks! I used to dread the inevitable moment when, while holding up a dress I'd fallen in love with, a friend or friendly salesperson would encourage me to "Just try it on!" Sometimes I would, and when I did, it never, ever fit. Like not even *close*. I'd get stuck, or break a zipper, or rip fabric just trying to get the damn thing off. Picture me, sweating, stuck inside a T-shirt, with a salesperson standing outside the curtain asking, "Is everything okay in there?" YOU KNOW IT IS NOT OKAY IN HERE BECAUSE I AM MAKING THE SAME NOISE AS A ROCKETSHIP REENTERING THE ATMOSPHERE. It was always so embarrassing. It made me want to shrivel up into a slug of shame.

However, as I became increasingly more comfortable sharing what I previously found embarrassing (and remember, that didn't happen overnight, it was part of the whole ~journey~), I decided to start sharing half-naked pictures of myself in dressing rooms with eeny-weeny dress-waists around my neck, my calves stuck in a pair of pants made for a tiny baby—the store's largest sizes, mind you. With each photo I posted on social media, I'd tag the brand, call them *in,* and beg them to #makemysize. Please!

This became my way of blocking that asshole dressing room lurker, Shame. Rather than berate myself endlessly for not fitting into a brand's clothes, I ask the brand, via public forum so they know that it's not just me asking, "Hey! Could you please make your cool clothes in more inclusive sizing? I'd love to wear them! A lot of us would!"

Two amazing things have come from the #makemysize hashtag: First, brands have listened. There have been numerous designers and labels who have said "You know what, you're right" and then actually *increased their sizing.* There have also been brands who have responded that they're listening and they're working on it. When they mean it, I really do appreciate it, and I genuinely look forward to seeing progress. But the best part of this whole thing has been all the amazing women who've started to share *their* dressing room experiences and asking brands to make *their* sizes, too. If using the hashtag empowers you and keeps Shame at bay, it's yours.

It's totally
to let som
to you du
body acce

adventu

normal

ething get

ng your

ptance

e.

Chapter Six

Family Tradition

ENuFs (see page 130) aren't the only ones to ride our ass about looking a certain way. This is going to sting, but I think we both know what's coming:

All too often, we're body-SHAMED by the very people we hold close inside our inner circle.

Allow me to run through a small selection of my own experiences for nostalgia's sake:

1. My whole life, I've had family members, friends, and romantic partners tell me different versions of "You'd be so pretty if you lost weight," or "You'll lose the weight when you're ready," or straight-up "When are you going to lose some weight?"

2. One year of my life, in my early twenties, I started obsessively trying to lose weight. At my lowest, I weighed a hundred pounds less than I do right now, and it was a struggle to keep the number there. I was on an excruciatingly restrictive and definitely not-healthy diet. I worked out so often that there's no way my body ever had a chance to recover. I was always miserable, tired, and hungry—and yet my family commended me for having this body.

3. Once, at a family birthday party, my ex's aunt pointed out that I have "big legs," then told me she wouldn't know what to do with them. Like, good thing they're mine and not yours, then, lady. I don't know what to tell you.

4. Speaking of exes, I have an ex who used to constantly make me feel bad about my body. He'd tell me I looked gross (only he'd hide his diss in a "we," as in, "*We* are getting gross; time to lose some weight"). Any time I tried something new with my style, or wore something that showed off skin, he'd make comments that implied I didn't realize how bad I looked, and that I was delusional for even attempting to dress that way.

Other things men have said to me:

- **"You should get gastric bypass.** Just do it. You'll be so much hotter if you do."

- **"Your face is so pretty.** Why don't you want to tone up your stomach?" (You'll notice this is also listed under "Other Common Words and Phrases, Along with 'Brave,' That Make Me Roll My Eyes," page 166.)

- **"Have you ever tried yoga?** I think your body would take to it well."

I worked for a woman who asked point-blank: "What are you eating every day?" It's a wonder she didn't just ask "So Katie, why are you so fat?"

Her question came out of nowhere, but I remember being so proud of my response: "Vegetables and ice cream." Power move, right?

"Why don't you try eating more vegetables and less ice cream," she replied, as my confidence deflated like a spit-covered balloon.

Because these people are close to us—whether they're close emotionally, physically, professionally, and/or via family tree— their put-downs sting even harder and cut even deeper than those of the ENuFs, and they leave a much longer-lasting impression. If the people we trust the most are telling us there's something wrong with our body, well, why wouldn't we believe them?

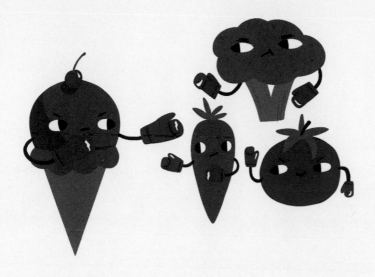

The hardest thing to understand in all of this—but I think it's crucial to say, particularly where loved ones are concerned—is that, in many of these cases, these people in your inner circle don't realize they're being total assholes. They don't realize that they're hurting you. They think they're *helping* you—they care about your well-being, after all. <u>What helps me not lose my ABSOLUTE SHIT when someone close to me makes a comment about my weight is to remember three things:</u>

1. They want me to be happy.

2. Because of their own hang-ups, experiences, ENuFs, relationships, and generally fat-phobic social conditioning, they don't understand that my weight doesn't add to or subtract from my value. My appearance doesn't determine my self-worth.

3. This is their problem. Not mine.

It still STINGS, though.

When my family makes comments about my weight, it's frequently wrapped in the hard-to-argue-with-because-I'm-not-a-doctor question "What about your health?" Well, what about my health? I am physically active. I eat vegetables—more vegetables than ice cream, if you can believe it, even though that former boss of mine could not.

"What about your cholesterol?" they've wanted to know. My cholesterol is fine, thank you very much. If pushed beyond that, I tell them:

- I have a doctor I trust and visit for yearly physicals.

- I wake up each day absolutely raring to go.

- I feel strong.

- I have stamina and energy.

- I move my body (sometimes it's a super sweaty workout. Other times it's a nice walk around the block with an iced coffee in one hand and my dogs' leashes in the other).

- I feed my body.

- I have regular bowel movements.

- I meditate *and* floss every day.

- I do not floss every day. That was a lie.

- There is no singular "healthy body type."

Then I ask for permission to nose through their recent medical history. They seem to shut up at that point.

Your health is a personal matter.

<u>My advice:</u> Take it seriously, find doctors you trust, nourish your body, move your body, be kind to your body. And always wear a seatbelt, even if you're sitting in the back!

DON'T BLAME
THE MOMS

I love my mom. She is the most special, incredible woman I know. She is kind and caring, smart and thoughtful, gentle and wonderful and nurturing. She's active in a garden club, a book club, and a French club. She takes sailing lessons and has gotten really good! She travels the world. This woman is not dependent on anyone for her happiness. She is entirely in charge of her life, and I love that about her. I am who I am today because of her—but therein lies the complicated part of a daughter's relationship with her mother: Whether we are of them or from them, similar or polar opposites, we are two individuals who were raised in very different worlds, at very different times.

Translation: It's normal to love the woman you call Mom, and to be simultaneously infuriated by her incessant poking and prodding at your gut. The thing is, there's a good chance she grew up in a household where *her* appearance was commented on. But just because it's generational doesn't mean it's "right." That's why we're here, today, to work on that. So that we don't pass negative body energy on to the next generation.

My mom is among the loved ones who make comments about my body. She always has, and while I've never faulted her for it, it's always been a high hurdle to jump. How am I supposed to accept my shape and weight and being if the very woman who created me can't? What about when I do accept my body . . . how do I accept the fact that my mom does not?

She grew up in an all-female household in which comparing and critiquing bodies was the usual. Her nickname was "Skinny." She had a twenty-four-inch waist when she married my dad. Today, in her early seventies, she's still thin. Growing up, I never felt like I could talk to her about my size because of the endless comments she made. I didn't think she would understand what it was like.

She wouldn't, is likely the honest answer. I don't think she does, even today. But what I didn't understand as a kid and a teen and even a twentysomething is that my mom has her own deep-rooted insecurities, too. How could she not? All of us have been conditioned to believe our bodies are never-ending works in progress—that, as women, we're never good enough, fit enough, thin enough, smooth enough, young enough, hairless enough, dainty enough—the list goes on. Remembering this fact helps me to feel compassion toward my mom. With no body positivity community to turn to at any point in her life, she has had to endure far worse ENuFs than I have—and she's had to endure them alone. It's not like she and her friends have a habit of talking about these things. If anything, the way they bond is to criticize their respective weights and diet failures and sweet tooths. Now that I'm older, I realize her comments toward me were her way of trying to help. She wanted me to be smaller because she believed it would make my life easier. So, when our moms, or our grandmas, or our aunts, or other female authority figures, role models, or caretakers make comments about our body not being *whatever* enough, it's not their fault. I truly believe that. They're trying to help shield us from the pain they've felt. Or feel. They're trying to teach us what they've been taught. What they know. To them, it's all part of being a woman.

Lucky for us, we know that being a woman means we have the power within ourselves to throw these archaic, bullshit mindsets out the window.

Recognizing Red Flags

It's not always easy to identify who in our inner circle is making us feel like crap. I mean, you think it would be easy: An insult is an insult, right? But the reality is that so many of these interactions take place under the covert disguise of friendly banter, faux solidarity, and backhanded compliments. I will never forget the time I was at a dinner party and the host—a very thin woman with gravel-driveway abs who was practically born on a Pilates reformer—pointed out my "athletic frame" to the entire dinner table.

"I bet my shoulders are bigger than yours," she challenged. "Let's compare."

She then had us stand back to back, in front of everyone, so that we could see who had the bigger shoulders. Obviously, I was going to have the bigger shoulders. The whole thing was insane. Later, fellow guests told me they, too, thought it was insane. But the craziest part is that I didn't *think* it was insane until other people pointed out that it was. Until then, I'd merely been wallowing in a quiet pool of body shame, feeling like an enormous snail, wishing I could just disappear. (Cue the balloon-fart noise of my confidence deflating.)

We're so used to feeling bad about our bodies that it doesn't always register when we're being made to feel even worse about ourselves. We're taught to laugh at ourselves so that we're in on the joke, not the punch line—even when our butt is the butt of the joke. We're expected to be polite even when others are being rude—for example, when the host of a party asks us to compare shoulders in front of an entire dinner table. We're made to believe that feeling like shit about our body is our own fault—after all, *we're the ones who look this way.* But I'm here to tell you that we feel like shit about our body because OTHER PEOPLE make us feel like shit about our body.

The good news is that learning to recognize when a friend's "joke" is actually a backhanded compliment, or when a family member's "concern for your health" is really just a fifteen-minute soapbox performance of negative body commentary, helps us separate their junk from our own. Their problem with your body is *their* problem.

OTHER COMMON WORDS AND PHRASES (ALONG WITH "BRAVE") THAT MAKE ME ROLL MY EYES

FLATTERING: "Flattering" is a euphemism for clothes that make you look thinner than you really are. "Unflattering" is a euphemism for clothes that showcase "the bad kind of fat." So when someone tells me a dress is "flattering" on my figure, or comments that the shorts I'm wearing are "unflattering" on my legs, what I hear is "That dress makes you look smaller than you really are, which is a good thing," and "Those shorts make you look fat—and there's something wrong with that."

Instead of "flattering," I encourage family and friends to say "THAT LOOKS AMAZING ON YOU, KATIE STURINO."

Instead of "unflattering," I encourage family and friends to not say anything unless their opinion was specifically requested. In the odd case that it *was* specifically requested, I hope they know me well enough to say something like "Those shorts aren't my favorite. I prefer the other ones, but go with the ones that make you happy. That's all that matters."

"YOU HAVE SUCH A PRETTY FACE!" What I hear is "But your body is a mess." Or worse, "YOU'D BE SO PRETTY IF YOU JUST LOST A LITTLE WEIGHT." Oh, wow, thanks!!! (???) "OUR SIZES DON'T GO THAT HIGH, BUT WE DO HAVE A 12 YOU COULD TRY."

When I can't find my size in a store, I do appreciate when the salesperson clearly wants to help. After all, it's not their fault the designer doesn't make my size or that the store has chosen not to carry it. But I often want to be like, "Dude, look at me. You and I both know I'm not fitting into that size 12. So why put me through the shame of getting stuck in a dressing room clothing trap?"

Take some time to reflect on common interactions with people inside your inner circle that make you feel crappy. Is there one person in particular who tends to bring you down? Do you get piled on in a group setting? Does it feel intentional and cruel, or do these people truly have your best interests at heart?

These are hard questions to ask yourself, particularly when people you love are involved. But they're important truths to identify. Once you can pinpoint the roots of your negative body feelings, you can start to pull those weeds out.

THE GARDENER'S GUIDE TO BODY NEGATIVITY WEEDING

Identifying a Weed
If someone or something makes you feel bad about your body, it is a weed.

Determining the Type of Weed
If the weed's negativity feels deliberate and intentionally mean and you'd rather not have the weed in your life, I'm inclined to tell you to chuck it. Proceed to "Pulling a Weed," opposite.

If the weed's negativity seems to be subconscious and you know the weed to be an otherwise important and loving figure in your life, then you should try replanting.

Pulling a Weed

If a weed needs to be pulled, you have a few options:

1. You can tell the weed you've had enough of their shit and unless they're ready to stop making your body their business, you never want to hear from them again.

2. You can ask your other friends for support. Something like, "Hey, pal? Could you help me change the subject if our third group chat member starts asking me about my diet again?"

3. You can excuse yourself from the table, the conversation, the topic at hand. You can opt out at any time, and guess what? You don't ever have to opt back in.

The overall goal is to protect yourself from the intrusive negativity of others, just as you would protect your mascot from a big bully. If you find yourself worrying that you can't possibly defend yourself in this kind of scenario, stand up a little straighter, crack your back, then ask yourself a question: "How would I defend my mascot? What can I do, right now, to protect that cartwheeling child inside me?"

Replanting a Weed

To replant a weed, start with a talk. The next time this person says something that hurts your feelings—or better yet (but much harder), *before* they have a chance to say something that hurts your feelings—pull them aside and let them know how their words make you feel. Set boundaries around what you do and don't find funny. Express what your expectations are for the relationship, and hear out whether their expectations align. The ones worth replanting will take your conversation to heart. The ones who don't, well, bye.

REMEMBER ONE THING

While I sincerely believe people can change—I've seen it happen—it's not your responsibility to change them. It is, however, your responsibility to protect yourself from what makes you feel like shit. Do what you will with that information.

LOOKING

FORWARD

You've Got Your Brain
Space Back! Now What
Will You Do with It?

Now What? (Asking for a Friend)

Meditation
Picking up tennis (even though you're bad at it)
Learn to cook like Julia Child
Quitting your job and joining the CIA
Finding love at the grocery store
Become someone who kayaks
Run for local office (or your office's baking committee)
Deepening friendships
Hopping on a plane
Calling your mom
Getting into fancy soap
Learning Mandarin
Shame
Thinking about what you just ate
Counting calories

Once you realize your power, what will you do with it?

The changes we've been talking about and working through don't just happen overnight. This process is about the gradual strengthening of the power, confidence, and self-worth that's always existed within you.

It is my hope that you have moments throughout this journey and beyond where you look at yourself in the mirror post-shower and think, "Oh my god. Wow. I finally see it: My body is a divine, awe-inspiring collection of cells that needs to be either carved into the side of a mountain or painted in the nude by a famous artist *immediately.*"

Just as important, if not more so, is that you start to appreciate your body for being a body, for all the hard and incredible work it does for you; that you find ways to be amazed by its ability to function, just in general; that you feel compelled to write about it in your gratitude journal just because it exists, and because you exist within it—all while simultaneously learning to detach the concept of "VALUE" from your appearance.

It is <u>OKAY</u> to be rendered speechless daily

by the BEAUTY
of your body.

It is okay that your self-determined "flaws" do not turn you on. It is okay to look in the mirror and acknowledge your flesh, give it a chin nod, and then move on with your day. It is okay to feel "meh." You have other, far more important things to fill your time with. You are worthy of this world, end of conversation. What you look like has nothing to do with it.

You know how moms are allowed to tell their kids "Because I said so" as a definitive answer that shuts down any further questions, Your Honor?

Well, if your mascot starts asking "But *why*," go ahead and tell her: You are worthy because I said so. You are worthy because you are worthy because you are worthy.*

Once I began to understand all THIS, an overwhelming desire to tell other women about it began burbling up in my stomach (in a good way). The feeling was similar to the moment I realized my anxiety and depression medication was working: You're telling me

---

* By the fourth "worthy," the word will start to sound weird, so you may need to cause a diversion to change the subject.

You are

WORTHY

of this

WORLD

I *don't* have to walk around feeling like shit? Really? You're telling me I can think about the things I'd rather be thinking about? That I can focus my energy on things I'd rather be doing? Are you telling me that I can be happy? That I can ditch that douche Shame and hang out instead with my cool friend Confidence?

That's why I do what I do. That's why I can't shut the hell up about this stuff!

And when Shame does try to get back together?

<u>Here's a quick story on that:</u> While writing this book, all high and hopped up on the opportunity to spread the gospel of body acceptance, I ran into someone from my past on the street.

Seeing this person, because of his connection to a pretty painful part of my life—a time when I was ashamed about who I was because I was ashamed about what I looked like—caused me to spiral hard and fast. We stopped and chatted as if it were no big deal while my insides threatened to start working on a mean diarrhea attack. I told this guy what I was "up to," and he told me his version of the same. The interaction was not even five minutes long and so seemingly innocuous that you would have fallen asleep watching it on playback. But because I still associate this person with a toxic group of people, with his being cooler than I am, with his being "better" than I am, with his having power over me during a time when I didn't know my own power, I walked away feeling small and insignificant. Old thoughts came rushing back about how I was an unlovable ugly monster. How dare I want to feel successful, I suddenly thought. How embarrassing to think I could ever be anything great.

Cut to: Me crying like a baby on the streets of New York while walking to a meeting about this very book, then feeling ashamed for crying and feeling this way.

Get it together, Katie, I told myself. You are supposed to be OVER this! How can you talk to people about overcoming deep-rooted issues with their bodies when you're clearly not over your own?

The dirty feeling from that interaction wore off throughout the day. Slowly but surely, I began to calm down and return to my center. What calmed me was the funny realization that the dirty feeling from my interaction with that guy *WORE OFF AT ALL*. A few years ago, there was no "wearing off." I carried it around with

me always. That was how I operated. That was my neutral base. So the fact that it *returned,* even though it was a scary visceral flashback, meant that it was no longer always there. And the fact that it went away?—after waving my giant NOPE! flag and standing up for my mascot and practicing all the strategies we've talked about in this book—man, that was something to celebrate.

I tell you all of this because you will have completely crap days. That's okay. You are bigger than a crap day. You *will* work through it. Clap for your inner child. Acknowledge that she had a scary fall and that she's brave for standing back up.

The Positive Side Effects of Body Acceptance

As my perception of my body and self-worth began to change for the better, so, too, did a few major factors in my life.

1. LOVE!

I gained seventy pounds during my divorce. As I began to acquaint myself with the new size and shape of my body, <u>I was simultaneously reacquainting myself with what it meant to prioritize my wants, needs, and desires.</u> What I really wanted, I realized, was to be loved deeply and unconditionally. And I wanted to love deeply and unconditionally in return.

Naturally, I went where all modern humans go when they want true love: a dating app, rife with unsolicited dick pics, unwanted pen pals, and future ghosts. There were plenty of duds. There was plenty of fun, too.

And then, out of nowhere, I met the man who would become my husband. He loves my body. He thinks it is the hottest thing in the world, and I am so grateful for that. It is a wonderful thing to be desired and loved by the person you desire and love. But he has

MY PERSONAL LIST OF DATING DOs & DON'Ts

Let me just tell you something: On my dating app profile, I showed my body! I let the people know what was up. Either they were going to be attracted to me or they weren't. Not my problem either way. I put it all out there from the get-go, which helped me cut right through the bullshit.

If you're considering entering the world of dating (for the first time in a long time, for the first time ever, doesn't matter), the most important thing is that you do what feels most comfortable to you.

Do: Embrace who you are in this moment.

Don't: Hide.

Do: Swipe front to back to avoid irritation. (That's a dating app/ toilet paper joke. I'll be here all night, folks.)

Don't: Listen to anyone, including the voices in your head, that may cause you to believe you have to look a certain way, or that you have to have completed some grand emotional transformation to find love. You are worthy of love right this very second, and the one after that.

Do: Tell Shame to go fuck himself if he's making you feel bad about putting yourself out there. He's just mad that he's not getting any. Not your problem.

shown me that he loves my body *because* he loves me, not that he loves me *because of my body*. It's like a sexy side effect. And he has shown me that he loves *me,* Katie, regardless of how I'm feeling about my body. He has shown me that I am worthy of love, that I did not—I do not—have to fix myself, body, or mindset to deserve his love.

You do not either.

You do NOT have to fix yourself to deserve love.

You do not have to alter your weight.

You do not have to do *any* of the work in this book if you don't want to. You deserve love and affection just because you exist.

2. New Friendships!

I made a lot of new friends as I began to accept my body.
Friendships ended during this time, too.

Not everyone will be comfortable with your newfound confidence.
It is possible that people who were part of your "old" life simply
won't be able to adjust to your new life. It doesn't mean they're
bad people. It just means that your energies are no longer a fit.
And guess what? That is very much not your problem.

As I began to accept my body, I stopped embracing my role
as the butt of all jokes, as the lesser-than wingwoman whose
sole purpose was to make my friends look more desirable in
comparison. I was sick of being the friend who always gave boosts
but never got boosted. When I finally did start to ask for boosts,
not everyone was on board. The real ones were, of course. The real
ones were like, "Oh my god, of course. Hold on two seconds while
I set up this enormous ladder." But some were uncomfortable
that I wanted a level playing field, which hurt. It hurt even
worse because, at the time, I thought they were real friends and
I worried that maybe I'd done something wrong. That was just
that old dick Shame talking. Shut up, Shame. Once I distanced
myself from those not-real friendships, I suddenly had the time
to make and develop relationships in my life that are enriching,
empowering, and *worthy of both our time.*

3. Style!

One of the best things to ever happen to my style was deciding that the word "flattering" was useless. Flattering according to whom? And to what rule book?

I love being naked. I think I'd really thrive in a nudist colony. Just ask my neighbors.* But once I stopped believing that my body had to be a certain size, shape, and weight to "pull something off," I started having fun getting dressed.

Many full moons ago, I bought a mint green shearling coat. It was comically puffy. I looked like a stuffed animal in it, and I loved it. I thought it was cool. I still think about it. I ended up returning it because so many people said to me, "You're already big. You don't need *more* volume." One person—who I should have listened to— said: "This coat isn't meant to be 'flattering.' This coat is meant to make a statement. It's meant to make you happy. If you like the coat, keep the coat." So when it comes to style, that's my new mantra: If I like it, I wear it. It's that simple.

My wish for you is that you find your own version of that mantra. (Feel free to use mine since it's easy to remember.) Ask yourself,

---

* If anyone wants to start an all-bodies-welcome nudist colony on the beach somewhere, let me know. I'll bring a thigh chafe stick and sunscreen.

"What inspires me? What do I want to say today? How do I want to feel?" Wear what makes you feel good.

If it feels scary to suddenly start wearing the wild things you've dreamed about after a lifetime of covering up insecurities (I so get that), allow yourself the space to ease into this. Pick *one* thing and try it. Wear it around the home when you're alone. Take some selfies. Put it on again tomorrow, and this time, leave the house. Walk down the block in it. Run one errand in it. Baby steps. Really, really well-dressed baby steps.

Just remember: You don't have to wait until you reach a goal weight. You don't have to wait for some extreme makeover. You don't have to wait for a special event, a birthday, or a vacation.

This is your moment.
GO FOR IT.

(Tomorrow's your moment, too, but unless you were about to take a power nap, what are you waiting for?)

"Just remember: You don't have to wait
until you reach a goal weight."

4. My Career!

When I started MegaBabe, it was because I wanted to make something that was a tangible extension of my body acceptance message to help remove shame around things we don't need to be shameful of.

Remember that version of me who felt like a bear in poopy sweats around svelte magazine editors? She never would have started a product line that made anti-chafing sticks. To her, that would have been a public admission of having thighs that rub together in a world where she felt like the only person without a thigh gap. Now I can't even imagine a world where I don't apply my anti-chafing sticks to the inside of my thighs in public, then post a video of myself doing so to the internet.

You do not have to start a company to prove your body acceptance progress. You don't have to do anything you don't want to. Remember? You don't have to do shit.

But! If you've been thinking about something, dreaming about an ice cream store, let yourself talk about it. Just tell one person. Allow yourself to dream beyond the limitations you long ago set for yourself. See where it leads you. Allow your friends to get excited when you let them in on secret ambitions. Brainstorm. See where that gets you. Play around a little bit. Think about what your personal definition of success means, then let yourself go for it head on.

SELL YOUR FAILURE DRESS

A failure dress is that dress (or top, or maybe it's a pair of jeans) that is way, way too small, yet you hold on to it anyway. I used to think of this kind of clothing as a goal marker: "If I can fit into these shorts, it means I've finally reached my goal weight." Once, back when I weighed a whole lot less than I do now (this was back when I worked in fashion PR and had to attend all those magazine desksides I told you about on page 75), I bought a VERY EXPENSIVE designer dress that was laughably tight and barely zipped—the last one they had. I was determined to make it work. I wore it until I no longer fit in it, but I kept it in the hopes that it might encourage me to buckle down and lose the weight again. The dress encouraged me, sure, but not in a healthy way: I prayed for the stomach flu and food poisoning to kick-start my weight loss. I vowed to skip meals and to salute the grumbling complaints from my stomach. I ended up gaining weight. And as the years went on, the dress continued to sit in my closet, collect dust, and taunt me. Talk about a trigger for all the negative things I used to say to myself. This dress was a daily reminder of an arbitrary goal I'd failed to achieve, and it made me feel bad every time I looked at it.

The day I decided to sell the dress was transformative (I'm not even being dramatic). Clearing that one dress out of my closet was better than any clothing purchase I've ever made. It created space in my mind to get creative with the clothes hanging there that did fit.

I highly recommend this step if you're looking for a mood boost. Sell your failure dress. Your mascot will thank you for it.

What Do YOU Want to Do?

As you start to embrace your body and the confidence that comes with it—not to mention the brain space that'll be freed up once you're not busy obsessing about your "flaws" all day—start asking yourself what you want to do with that power and cranial real estate. Do you want to travel more? Quit your job and pursue your passion? Stay at your job and get promoted to partner? Do you want to learn another language? Take a dance class? A history class? Do you want to paint more? Bake more? Do you want to take a walk on the beach in a thong-bottom swimsuit without thinking twice about your cellulite?

<u>Start writing some of those things down. Right now!</u> Here, I provided an entire blank page for you to begin your list.

ALL THE THINGS I WANT TO DO NOW THAT MY BRAIN IS FREEEEEEEE!

THE BENEFITS OF
Being Big

As part of my body acceptance journey, I started writing out "The Benefits Of" lists. I focus on things that the old me would have talked shit about, like being big, and instead, I write a kind of gratitude list for each thing. Some days these lists are liberating, some days these lists feel true, and some days I write them purely to make myself laugh.

If you're having a shit-talking kind of day, why not try making your own "Benefits Of" list right now? Write it down here. No pen within reach? Toss some ideas around in your head. I encourage you to try this.

In fact, why not use the next page? I left it blank for you. I'll go first.

THE BENEFITS OF BEING BIG

- I always have a great view of the stage.
- I can rearrange my own furniture without any help.
- I can reach anything on any shelf.
- I rarely have to make more than one trip when carrying groceries from my car to the front door.
- It'd be hard to knock me over in a stampede.
- I'm not easily jostled on the subway.
- I can lift my own luggage.
- I'm an eager masseuse's dream. Lotta real estate to cover.
- It feels really good to hug me because I'm soft and squishy, like a memory foam mattress.
- For my husband, there's more of me to love.
- I am a king-size bed for my dogs.
- I cast an enormous shadow, which means I'm never alone.
- I stand out in a crowd.

WRITE YOUR BENEFITS OF _____ LIST HERE

{Your answer here}

_____

_____

_____

_____

_____

_____

_____

_____

_____

_____

_____

_____

_____

_____

_____

_____

_____

You are BIGGER than a crap day.

(Don't worry, this test is open-book. And yes, you can use your notes.)

Remember when (on page 110) I asked you to write out some of the arbitrary limitations you'd previously placed upon yourself because of body shame? "I can't wear/do _____ because _____."

Think about the items on that list. Do they still feel un-doable? Well, they very much ARE doable, just so we're on the same page. I'll prove it: I challenge you to do or wear the very thing you said you couldn't. You don't have to make it a Thing. You don't have to tell the whole world about it. Just try it—even a *teeny, tiny* piece of it.

Do you hear that? Your mascot is cheering. I bet she's so damn proud.

"You can wear these!"

Chapter Eight

Pass It On

You've made it. You're armed with the tools to free up your mental space from body negativity. You know how to block ENuFs and weed your inner circle. You're learning to speak to yourself with more kindness and to stop equating your appearance with your self-worth. You know how to say NOPE! to junk food thoughts, and you're working on saying yes to your dreams. You are the official protector of your mascot—who is, of course, you—and in doing so, you are healing the young girl within you who now knows, without a shadow of a doubt, that she is worthy. You have read and said the word "worthy" so many times now that it sounds weird and you can't even be sure we're spelling it correctly. That's amazing!

- **"WAIT, BUT KATIE, I DON'T THINK I'M AS FAR ALONG AS YOU THINK I AM. I AM STILL LEARNING."**

  I know! So am I.

- **"I THINK I NEED TO STUDY MORE."**

  Every day *is a study in building up our own self-confidence. Some days are better than others, remember?*

- **"I HAVEN'T DONE ANY OF THE HOMEWORK YET! I SKIPPED AHEAD IN THE BOOK BECAUSE YOU SAID I COULD AND NOW I'M LIKE, 'AHHHHHHHH!'"**

  You are doing your homework right now, just by being here. Just by being cognizant of the fact that you want to start accepting your body and being intentional about your next moves, you are changing energy within yourself.

You have the POWER to change the energy AROUND you, too.

When speaking to the next generation of women—as well as our own and the ones before us—what do you say we tell them everything we wish we were told ourselves?

- Let's tell them how smart, strong, clever, funny, and confident they are, *in addition* to celebrating and complimenting their unique-to-them beauty.

- Speaking of beauty, what do you say we drive home, early on in life, right from the start, to all members of the next rising and future generations, that beauty—while theirs is lovely and sunny and wonderful as is—really does shine from within.

- Let's teach them to embrace the individual beauty of our physical differences.

- Let's encourage, as well as demonstrate, empathy and kindness toward all humans.

- Finally, let's champion the wacky hopes and wild dreams of all those who deem us special enough to hear them.

When I was writing this book, I couldn't help but think about all the things I wish I'd been told growing up, and how differently I might have approached my relationship with myself had I known then what I do now. Certainly, I would have been kinder to myself and far more gracious to my body. I wish I had known that my weight didn't define me. I wish I'd learned to have empathy earlier on for the women in my life who don't want to see me struggle with my weight the way they did.

Growing up, I wish I had known that just because magazines or movies or mean bullies on the playground had a narrow view of what beauty meant didn't mean I had to adopt that view.

I wish I'd learned so much sooner that how much I weigh has nothing whatsoever to do with who I am.

I wish I had known that none of that had or has the ability to make me ineligible for the many joys of life. I wish I had known that I was worthy. That I am worthy.

To the little girl inside me, my mascot, bold defender of my self-esteem, and to all the inner children and full-grown adults of my and future generations (who just so happen to be reading this),

I promise you the following:

Your body—in all its unique and wondrous glory; in all its curves and curls and swerves and pockets of fat; with all its jiggles and hairs, scars and scrapes, lumps, bumps, dents, bruises, and future stretch marks that tell the story of skin well lived in; with all its idiosyncratic DNA strands that link you to your family tree—all of it is beautiful. There is nothing at all wrong with you. There is only everything right.

It's time to pass the message along. I bet your mascot could use a few other mascots to play with. Now go pick your wedgie and enjoy doing donkey kick cartwheels to your heart's content.

There is
at all wro
you. The
everythir

nothing

g with

e is only

g right. ♥

Acknowledgments

Amelia Diamond: I owe everything to you, starting with the fact
that this book is real. If you hadn't said yes that day, I would never
have started my blog. When I got overwhelmed about starting a
blog, you told to me to "just start with an Instagram account" and
called it a micro blog. You never yelled at me during this book
process even when I was the group project partner nobody wants
to have. Thanks for having the same upper face as me.

My parents are wonderful parents. Mom, you haven't done
anything wrong here. You didn't invent diet culture, and no
one is equipped to deal with a child who is five feet seven in
second grade. You did great! I wrote a book! (Two, actually!) I do
everything to make you proud. I love you.

Dad, when I finally got my mustache waxed when I was fourteen,
I will never forget coming home after and sitting down in
awkward silence, which you broke by saying, "You get that from
my side of the family."

Jenny, my sister. No one pushes me harder than you. You are
my biggest fan, and I'm so glad we decided to start a business
together so we can talk forty-two times a day. I love you even when
I hate you.

John Sturino. The newest Sturino. I pinch your ear every day to see if you are real, and then I look around and wonder how anyone allows two full-grown babies to live by themselves. With bank accounts and everything. I will never stop being grateful for you. I love you.

Alyssa Reuben, thank you for always pushing me. For listening to my crazy book ideas with a straight face. And for always knowing I have more to say. I truly would not have done this book without you.

Amanda Englander: You made this book happen. You saw something special in this message and recognized that it was something that needed to be shared. You have vision. And a new puppy named Georgie, who I wish could have been my coauthor on this book so I could stare at him. Thank you for your thoughtful edits and your passion to help women feel better about their bodies.

Gabrielle Van Tassel: Having you in the room when we pitched this book made me understand that this book needed writing. You are the woman I am writing this for. The woman who gets it to the core. I am so grateful you wanted to be on this project!

To the team at Clarkson Potter, Ian Dingman, Terry Deal, and Kim Tyner, thank you for all of your loving care, thrilling creativity, brilliant expertise, and generous amounts of time spent on making this come to life. It was an honor to work with each and every one of you!

Published in the United States by Clarkson Potter/
Publishers, an imprint of the Random House
Publishing Group, a division of Penguin Random
House LLC, New York.

clarksonpotter.com

CLARKSON POTTER is a trademark and POTTER with
colophon is a registered trademark of Penguin
Random House LLC.

Library of Congress Control Number: 2020942517

ISBN 978-0-593-23212-5
Ebook ISBN 978-0-593-23213-2
Printed in China

WRITER: Amelia Diamond
ILLUSTRATOR: Monica Garwood
EDITOR: Gabrielle Van Tassel
DESIGNER: Laura Palese
PHOTOGRAPHER (BACK COVER): Jamie Magnifico
PRODUCTION EDITOR: Terry Deal
PRODUCTION MANAGER: Kim Tyner
COPY EDITOR: Mary Anne Stewart

10 9 8 7 6 5 4 3 2 1

First Edition